WHY
PRIDE
MATTERS MORE
THAN MONEY

■

*The Power
of the World's Greatest
Motivational Force*

JON R. KATZENBACH

CROWN
BUSINESS
NEW YORK

Published by Crown Business, New York, New York.
Member of the Crown Publishing Group, a division of
Random House, Inc.
www.randomhouse.com

CROWN BUSINESS is a trademark and the Rising Sun colophon
is a registered trademark of Random House, Inc.

Printed in the United States of America

Design by Robert Bull

Library of Congress Cataloging-in-Publication Data
Katzenbach, Jon R., 1932–
Why pride matters more than money : the power of the world's
greatest motivational force / Jon R. Katzenbach.
Includes index.
1. Employee motivation. 2. Performance awards. 3. Pride and
vanity. 4. Psychology, Industrial. I. Title.
HF5549.5.M63 K377   2003
658.3'14—dc21   2002015939
ISBN 0-609-61065-1
10 9 8 7 6 5

First Edition

To Mom and Marvin

CONTENTS

Introduction   1
The Motivational Power of "Feeling Proud"

Chapter 1   21
Performance, Success, and Pride

Chapter 2   45
Money Talks; Materialistic Pride Listens

Chapter 3   69
Instilling Institution-Building Pride

Chapter 4   97
How Motivations Differ at the Front Line

Chapter 5   131
Instilling Pride—Peak Performance Environments

Chapter 6   151
Instilling Pride—Traditional Work Environments

Epilogue   179
A Learnable Skill

Acknowledgments   201

Index   205

WHY
PRIDE
MATTERS MORE
THAN MONEY

INTRODUCTION
The Motivational Power of "Feeling Proud"

When it comes to providing the incentives that motivate employee performance, far too many organizations are between a rock and a hard place. On the one hand, many only think of and rely on pay-for-performance incentive plans that simply provide more money for accomplishing specific goals. On the other, most can't afford to offer high monetary incentives to motivate the broad base of employees. Below a certain echelon of management, the amount of money most employees can earn is limited. There is no denying that monetary rewards have motivational power. What is not well understood, however, is just how limited financial rewards by themselves are in developing the kind of emotional commitment that builds the long-term sustainability of any organization, whether for-profit corporation, nonprofit, or government agency. Money by itself is likely to produce self-serving behavior and skin-deep organizational commitment rather than the type of institution-building behavior that is characteristic of organizations like the Marines, The Home Depot, and Southwest Airlines.

What makes me so sure? I've studied hundreds of companies in many, many industries and have gained insight into what motivates people to form emotional attachments that go way beyond the amount of monetary compensation offered. Beyond my years of consulting, two special people—my mother and Marvin Bower—provided my compass for this book. Mom, of course, was a relentless guiding light during my early years. Marvin Bower, the principal founder of McKinsey & Company, Inc., became my North Star when I entered the world of business as a member of "the Firm."

MOM

Mom always said, "Virtue is its own reward." She also said, "Set your sights high—reach for the moon; even if you don't make it, you will fall among the stars, and I will still be proud of you." Of course Mom was right. Virtue and high achievement create feelings of pride that amply reward us for the unusual dedication and effort required. But pride is more than simply an emotional reward for high achievement; it also motivates us toward such achievement. Because justifiable feelings of pride are so extremely rewarding, the anticipation of those feelings is also very motivating. You do not have to wait for success to feel proud of what you are doing and why you are doing it. The best mothers instinctively know this and become masters of nourishing that anticipation to motivate their children.

The best leaders also know this and use that knowledge to motivate higher levels of employee performance than would otherwise be possible. Like the best mothers, they realize that the anticipation of feeling proud is a more powerful motivator than the anticipation of being punished. And, of course, they recognize two motivational dimensions: feeling proud of yourself, and having those you respect and admire feel proud of you. This book explores how leaders at any level in almost any organizational setting can motivate higher employee performance by capitalizing on the anticipation of feeling proud and making others proud, too.

As with most people, "making Mom proud of me" was behind my early efforts to perform well. She always made it clear what would make her proud of me—and what would not. And because she had unrealistically high expectations, her standards were tough to meet. When Mom was around, I had to toe the mark; when she was not, other influences sometimes led me astray—but never without pangs of conscience. And since I grew up with her influence almost always at hand, I never strayed too far. I was strongly motivated to do, and to feel proud of, what would make Mom proud.

For example, her influence was pervasive in my determination to work hard, since she believed that was better than being smart. She also shaped my motivation to pursue graduate degrees, since she spent over twenty-five years of her adult life in pursuit of a college degree—a classic role model showing me that education mattered. In my most vivid image of her, she's seated at an old Underwood typewriter banging out correspondence courses, week after week, year after year. It is hard to overstate how proud she was when she marched down the aisle in cap and gown to get her degree at age fifty. Since I was still in high school at the time, I urged her to skip the cap and gown so as not to embarrass me. My embarrassment lasted about thirty seconds—until my eyes were filled with tears of pride and joy at what she had accomplished.

Mom's definitions of "success" were integral to what made her proudest of me—and they had much more to do with character than position or wealth. Not surprisingly, her definition of character encompassed a lot more than simply "telling the truth"; it meant treating others with trust and respect regardless of their position in life. And her definition of "courage" was precisely what I later discovered to be a guiding value for the Marines, i.e., "Do the right thing in the right way for the right reasons." Or, as she bluntly put it, "Speak up when you have something to say that you believe in—and be quiet when you have nothing to say that matters." There is little question in my mind that what I feel most proud of today stems from Mom's relentless and persistent attention to these simple basics. She defined success for me in terms that have stayed with me for life. I am sure that many readers have had a similar motivational "mom" in their early life.

But when I moved away from home, Mom's constant reinforcements faded, and my behaviors gradually changed. It became easier for me to rationalize modest deviations, and the lure of material possessions took over. I'm not sure I wanted to be conspicuously rich and famous, but I certainly wanted "more and better stuff"—not to mention the recognition that I felt would accompany that stuff. My dad ran a small business whose profits rarely exceeded $10,000 a year, and I was weary of living just above the poverty line. Sure, I remembered that Mom's values and feelings of pride had nothing to do with money; but, as I distanced myself from my childhood, her words had become intertwined with that time, and therefore I thought they were irrelevant to the complexities of adulthood I was encountering. About that time, fortunately, I joined the firm of McKinsey & Company, Inc., and a man by the name of Marvin Bower entered my life.

A SURROGATE MOM

I actually joined McKinsey for all the wrong reasons. First, the Firm—as many call it—was offering me a beginning salary of $9,600, which was among the higher offerings that year to graduates of the Harvard Business School. Second, they had an opening in San Francisco, and ever since my Stanford University days, I had dreamed of "living by the Bay" with the beautiful people. And last, I didn't think consulting was a "real job," so I planned on leaving McKinsey just as soon as I could find a more lucrative managerial position. Luckily for me, Marvin and his colleagues at McKinsey quickly clarified what were the right reasons for joining the firm: namely, serving worthy clients and growing professionally. Like my mother, Marvin was relentless in his zeal to clarify the performance philosophy that should motivate me—and much to my dismay, money was nowhere within it!

In one of my early encounters with Marvin, I was explaining how I had "lost" an opportunity to obtain a major piece of work with Memorex's CEO, Larry Spitters. I was simply unable to figure out how to help Larry organize his senior leadership group without first gaining an understanding of the economics and strategy of his business. Larry told me that would involve unnecessary extra work and turned down my proposal. Since I sounded a bit disappointed, Marvin was quick to point out why I should have been proud of realizing that I did not really have the capability to advise the CEO in the abstract. Marvin always thought we should be as proud of turning down work when we lacked distinctive capability as we were of obtaining work we were uniquely qualified to do. Nearly every one of my subsequent interactions with Marvin over our lengthy association has contained some "nuggets of wisdom" that have clarified for me what should make me feel proud—and what should not. While I didn't always agree, I never failed to gain insights about the most rewarding sources of pride.

What Marvin Bower influenced me to be proud of turned out to be pretty close to what Mom wanted me to be proud of—although the context and how they expressed it were somewhat different. Most important for you readers, however, is not what Marvin motivated me to take pride in. Rather, it is how he did it, namely, by enabling me to savor the pride that accompanies good professional work. He exemplifies what it takes to instill pride in performance among people who work with you. Perhaps even more important, he illustrates what it takes to instill the *anticipation* of being proud of your performance—far before the results produce pride all by themselves. My most recent visit with him illustrates once again why the most powerful motivation to perform is more about seeking to feel proud than seeking more money or materialistic gain.

REVISITING THE MASTER

It was a Saturday morning in June, and I was a bit nervous about my luncheon date with Marvin. Not only was he my former leader and mentor as managing director of McKinsey & Company, Inc.—he is (in my view) the "founding father" of the entire top-management consulting profession. It is difficult to identify very many true founding fathers in the world of major professional work, but when it comes to top-management consulting, Marvin is certainly as responsible as anyone for the profession. Before he teamed up with accounting professor James O. McKinsey to build McKinsey & Company into a top-management consulting firm, there was no identifiable profession beyond the individual counseling provided by a few leading academics and senior partners of law and accounting firms—or the time-and-motion-study experts. Marvin's vision of a professional firm devoted to helping corporate CEOs resolve the key leadership and management issues for their enterprises was the first of its kind. He paved the way for the countless strategic, leadership, and organization firms—both large and small—that exist today. He also launched and led the early efforts of the Association of Consulting Management Engineers (ACME) to establish a code (including values and capability requirements) for the profession. He stands alone as visionary, standard setter, and institution builder in the evolution of top-management consulting.

However, Marvin's early career interest was the law. He graduated from Harvard Law School in 1928 and applied for a job at Jones Day, one of the most prestigious law firms in Cleveland, Ohio. As he tells the story, he had not done well enough in law school for Jones Day to hire him, so he decided to go to the then fledgling Harvard Business School to strengthen his record. He was determined to work for a firm he knew he could be proud of, and upon graduation he joined Jones Day in their corporate law practice. From that auspicious beginning, he conceived the idea of top-management consulting—i.e., creating a firm that would bring the kind of professionalism and quality of work that he had found at Jones Day to the leadership and management issues of major corporations. Apparently, he reasoned that helping corporate leaders resolve their critical business issues *before the fact* would be a much more satisfying career than guiding them through their legal travails *after the fact*. Thus emerged the embryo of top-management consulting that eventually shaped McKinsey & Company, Inc., as well as the entire profession.

I consider myself extremely fortunate to have known Marvin for over forty years. I have worked with him in countless McKinsey client and Firm situations and still regard him as the ultimate role model and friend. Nonetheless, I was nervous about this lunch. Perhaps it was because I had not seen him since he'd lost his beloved wife, Cleo, and because my only contact with him for the past few years had been a couple of phone calls. Perhaps it was because I was no longer with McKinsey and wondered how he would view the consulting firm I had recently started; I still wanted Marvin to be proud of me. And perhaps it was because our mutual friend Mac Stewart had cautioned me that Marvin's age (ninety-eight) was finally catching up with him. What would he be like, what would he remember, what would we talk about? Simple enough questions, perhaps, but the circumstances were making me uneasy.

My flight arrived at the West Palm Beach airport nearly two hours in advance of our appointment. It was only a half-hour drive to Marvin's apartment, so I stopped for a cup of coffee in a quiet section of the airport to collect my thoughts. My mind wandered around the many wonderful memories I have of Marvin and how proud I was to have been associated with him. His first visit to the San Francisco office of McKinsey when I was a new associate stands out. He asked me to describe my one client assignment and was quick to point out both the good and the not-so-good aspects of my description.

His individual visits with me, however, were invariably warm and enjoyable. I reflected on the many times I had benefited from his unique style of "on-the-job coaching." He was direct—blunt even—which usually made me squirm. At the same time, it always made me resolve to try a bit harder the next time. He made it crystal clear what behaviors I should be proud of and which ones I needed to change. He was as transparent about his confidence in me as he was about his disappointment whenever he felt I might be "letting your partners down," as he phrased it. I also reflected on the times he had shared personal moments with my wife and me and conveyed feelings that only come with genuine caring. We always knew when he was proud of us, and we worked hard to justify his trust. My personal time with Marvin always brought out the best in me—and he took a sincere, personal interest in all aspects of my life.

Throughout my career, Marvin was a compelling role model of professionalism and character. While not perfect himself, he made perfection seem attainable. He set the example in both big and little ways. Certainly, he stood tall when confronting difficult clients in settings where others would have backed off. At the same time, he took great pride in attention to detail and doing the little things well. For example, he always wrote up his own interview notes, whereas most other partners would leave that task to the associates. He kept his own calendar, made his own appointments, edited his own documents, answered his own phone, placed his own calls, and corrected his own mistakes. Marvin seldom considered "leveraging his time" by making others do work that he could do. And most impressively, whatever Marvin said he would do, he did; he never had to be reminded of his commitments—large or small. As a role model for McKinsey associates, Marvin easily stands shoulder to shoulder with the U.S. Marine drill instructors, who are among the best role models in the world. And because he took such pride in attending to the details that produced high-quality, high-impact client work, the rest of us did, too.

As managing director of the Firm, Marvin's image was not only impressive but also sometimes intimidating. Feelings of anxiety often preceded his formal meetings with the office staff. For over half a century, he was larger-than-life to the associates and partners of McKinsey. To this day, some of the older directors of the Firm still resolve difficult issues by asking themselves, "What would Marvin do?" We all wanted Marvin to be proud of us. And we knew how proud we would feel when we did things he would be proud of—even though he might never know of them. It is hard to overstate the motivational impact of this mind-set.

At times I resented his bluntness, since it made it impossible for me to explain away or even justify behaviors that were less than exemplary. The look on his face alone was enough to tell you whether your behavior was acceptable. Moreover, since we all soon learned from Marvin what we should be proud of, we each disciplined one another accordingly in his absence. Just as at Marine boot camp at Parris Island, Marvin's top-down influence on our attitudes and behaviors gradually evolved into peer discipline and self-discipline. And when self-discipline kicks in, anticipatory pride takes over as the primary motivational force because you learn that you are actually capable of much more than you ever thought possible.

UNWARRANTED ANXIETIES

One of Marvin's nurses greeted me at the door of his apartment. She pointed to Marvin's study, where I could see him seated in a straight-backed chair facing away from the door. "So where is he hiding now?" I said loudly and playfully, hoping that a little early humor would break the ice. It seemed to work, since I could hear a familiar chuckle from the study that quickly moderated my anxiety.

As I entered the room, it was not Marvin's physical appearance or age that captured my attention. Instead, it was an all too familiar intensity in his gaze and sparkle in his eye. "Would you like to see the rest of the apartment?" he asked rhetorically. "It's all Cleo's doing, you know." As he reached for his shiny, chromium walker, he jokingly observed, "This is the Cadillac of walkers, but Cleo insisted I get it. I have to use it all the time now, but it is a lot better than being hauled everywhere in those little motor carts like most of my neighbors. At least I'm getting some exercise."

It was endearing and encouraging seeing how much Cleo had meant to him—and still means to him. I had worried that discussions of her would be sad, but again my fears were completely unfounded. Marvin's love for his second wife and his pride in her—as well as his interest in doing what she would be proud of—remains as strong as ever. Clearly, she remains a positive motivational force in his life.

We talked of many things as we toured the various rooms, e.g., old friends such as Al Gordon, founding partner of Kidder, Peabody (also approaching his one hundredth birthday); children, grandchildren, and great-grandchildren; and visits abroad that various tokens brought to mind.

Marvin was concerned about my wife's health, interested in the location of our new home, and curious about my new firm. Nothing escaped his notice or attention. Sometimes his responses were slow, occasionally unclear, but never irrelevant. Every now and then the name of a person or a place would escape him, but no more often than such things happen to me.

It was a healthy walk from Marvin's third-floor home at one end of the complex to the waterfront restaurant at the other end. Marvin introduced me to his favorite waiter, Benson, who said proudly that any friend of Mr. B's was a friend of his. Benson wondered if Marvin was my father, since the next day was Father's Day. "I'm afraid not," I said. "I had a wonderful father myself—but if it were possible to have a second one, Mr. B would be my first choice." We all chuckled a bit at that and settled down to lunch. I asked Marvin's advice on a number of issues concerning the development of my new firm (a bit hesitatingly, I'm afraid, since I wanted him to recognize why I was so proud of it). As usual, his advice was insightful and on the mark. However, when I asked about how he had inculcated basic values in the early days of McKinsey, he found the question puzzling. Values, to Marvin, were natural and intuitive; hence, he could not imagine a professional firm of any stature not having them internalized right from the beginning. How else could you possibly motivate people to do the right thing? I also asked him when and how he knew that McKinsey was headed for greatness. The answer, of course, was the same—he knew from the very beginning: "I had the benefit of working for a great professional firm [Jones Day] while I was forming my concepts and aspirations. . . . I knew what it was like, what the values needed to be. . . . I could never be satisfied with anything less."

I also wondered at what point in the early years of creating McKinsey & Company, Inc. he might have found it necessary to replace and upgrade his original group, who were mostly accountants. To my surprise, Marvin indicated that most of them proved able to "rise to the challenge" of what the Firm was building and doing. Their pride in the effort clearly motivated them to outperform normal expectations.

Of course, McKinsey & Company, Inc. was more important to Marvin than anything else in his life outside his immediate family. His pride in McKinsey never wavers, and that pride constantly motivates him, even at age ninety-eight, to urge his former partners to higher and higher levels of professional performance. And, of course, Marvin always expects the partners to "do the right thing in the right way for the right reason." While that is also the memorable motto of the U.S. Marine Corps, by far the best living model I know is Marvin Bower.

MOTIVATION AND PRIDE REKINDLED

One of the most interesting things I rediscovered during my last conversation with Marvin was how much I learn "around the edges" of his direct comments. But I have to listen carefully. While what he has to say is valuable, what is invariably more important are the informal context and "aura" of the discussion. And I usually had to reflect back on elements of our conversation to get the maximum learning benefits from any visit with him. This one was certainly no different in that respect, and I came away with renewed insights about how to instill pride in myself and those I work with:

- *Set aspirations that touch the emotions:* Impossible dreams are a source of pride even though they remain unachievable. No one really expects the Marines to win every battle and save every life—but that impossible dream is the fundamental underpinning of motivation in the Corps. Institutions with noble aspirations like the USMC have access to a powerful source of pride that permeates all parts of their organization.

- *Pursue a meaningful purpose:* Great organizations whose aspirations are not necessarily "noble" still pursue clear missions that provide a meaningful purpose for their people as well as to their customers and shareholders. They also adhere to a simple set of values that determine "how we do things around here." KFC's purpose of providing "affordable chicken dinners" is hardly noble, but they make it and their values meaningful to their people. As simple as it sounds, surprisingly few companies pay as much attention to their purpose and values as they do to their earnings. Those who do, however, are able to instill pride that can enable their people to perform in stormy as well as calm seas.

- *Cultivate personal relationships of respect:* Probably the most lasting benefits to be gained from a lifetime of work in different occupations come from the personal relationships of mutual trust and respect that one develops along the way. Along with family and friends, we want our respected workplace colleagues to be proud of us.

- *Become a person of high character:* Integrity, common courtesy, emotional commitment, and unassuming pride in group performance are the hallmarks of great human beings—not intellect, charisma, power, or personal gain. These traits also characterize great leadership accomplishment.

- *Look for the humor along the way:* As Mary Poppins said, "a spoonful of sugar helps the medicine go down." A sense of humor becomes increasingly indispensable as one gets older; perhaps it is the foundation of both wisdom and pride as well as enjoyment. Richard Cavanagh, an old friend and current CEO of the prestigious Conference Board, makes a point of not hiring people who lack a sense of humor; so do I. We both take considerable pride in having fun "professionally," a capability we developed into an art form under Marvin's wing.

WHAT THIS BOOK IS ABOUT

My simple visit with Marvin illustrates most of what I believe matters about motivation and pride. An intrinsic feeling of pride based on the relentless pursuit of worthwhile endeavors is a lasting and powerful motivating force. This kind of pride is also "institution-building" when it prompts the kind of effective, customer-focused behaviors that deliver quality products and economic performance. Conversely, feelings of pride based upon self-serving or materialistic gains are short-term, transient, and risky—such feelings tend to ebb and flow with the economic fortunes of those involved. They work fine when the winds of fortune blow favorably, but they disappear as soon as storm clouds gather.

Intrinsic or institution-building pride can take many forms—all of them deeply motivational. You can be proud of doing what people you respect will admire (parents, family, friends, colleagues, mentors, teachers, and heroes). You can also be proud of what you, yourself, know is uniquely good work—i.e., you can strive to create something of real and lasting quality, beauty, and durability—whether it is a painting, a symphony, a rose garden, or a professional firm. You can be proud of how you go about your work because you do it with intensity, integrity, concern for others, and attention to detail. Most important, you can be proud of simply creating unique opportunities for others that you like and respect, helping people around you to achieve their personal best. That kind of pride will clearly motivate you and others to perform at the highest levels over sustained periods.

The rest of this book builds on what I learned from Mom and Marvin about motivation and pride. It extends well beyond that set of early fundamentals and draws upon the experiences of some of the best frontline motivators I have worked with, known, and researched over my career as a writer and professional consultant to leaders in hundreds of different organizations. It is based upon the fundamental premise that leaders at any level who develop the capability to instill pride in others can use that ability to achieve higher levels of business performance. *Intrinsic or institution-building pride is the most important motivational element in a company for the following reasons:*

- Pride is more than an emotion that people only experience when they do something well. The anticipation of feeling proud is also a powerful motivating force that can be instilled beforehand. Moreover, what is required to instill institution-building pride is mostly teachable; the attitudes, approaches, and disciplines that instill pride constitute a managerial capability that can be made as fundamental as managing by the numbers. Those who master it can connect with the workforce, strengthen broad-based performance ethics, and reinforce achievement along multiple dimensions including economic, marketplace, and human or societal.

- A powerful "closed loop of energy" links pride to workforce performance and business success. Each element in the loop feeds upon the previous one in a mutually reinforcing cycle that results in higher and higher levels of business performance over time. It starts with the anticipation that higher performance will feel "good." Anticipating that feeling generates both energy and an emotional commitment to deliver better results. As those results contribute to recognized business success, the recognition instills strong feelings of pride—and the cycle repeats.

- This linkage applies to virtually every organization, public and private, large or small. The sources of pride may differ, and the tools and mechanisms can be diverse, but the fundamental connection between pride and performance applies in all areas of human organizational endeavor.

- Focusing on pride as the primary motivational element has important implications for how managers manage, how leaders lead, and how managers become leaders over time. Potential leaders at all levels can learn how to invoke pride in their people by triggering old memories, creating vicarious analogies, and sparking emotional anticipation of what lies ahead. You do not have to wait for tangible success to tap into the motivational power of pride.

Over time, pride matters more than money in motivating people to excel at whatever they do. When your employees take pride in doing those things that produce higher business results, your enterprise succeeds. When they take pride in self-serving activities that undermine business success, your enterprise flounders. At the same time, Maslow's hierarchy of human needs cannot be ignored. There is a baseline of monetary need and "fairness" beneath which motivation and pride will sink. When people are not paid enough to meet their fundamental human-safety and comfort needs, neither pride nor loyalty prevails.

The book clarifies important differences between self-serving and institution-building pride and illustrates why both work (but one is far better than the other as a lasting, motivating force). It will also illustrate the differences between what motivates the front line and what motivates top management, and why institution-building pride is more of an imperative throughout the broad base of employees. In addition, I will draw upon some recent research that identified the five paths followed by companies that excel at engaging the emotional commitment and pride of major segments of their workforce.

Most important, I believe that the book contains ideas and lessons for readers who work for companies where institution-building pride is not yet a capability nor a priority, but who want to begin using it to motivate their people. Cultivating pride as a motivational force for your organization is an investment that can yield high returns in workforce performance over time. Also, it is not likely to be as costly as relying primarily on monetary compensation and the turnover risks that accompany a "show me the money" culture. However, it does require senior leaders who believe in the motivational power of pride and are willing to encourage managers down the line to develop their pride-building skills. Pride-builders at or near the front line provide the critical connection for any organization that seeks to motivate its employees to excel.

CHAPTER 1

■

PERFORMANCE, SUCCESS, AND PRIDE

Pride is the emotional high that follows performance and success. The more interesting proposition, however, is that simple recollections of past "wins" and an empathy for the pride we sense in others (e.g., watching a sibling receive a special award) produce an anticipation of future "successes" that motivates performance. Moreover, success is in the eye of the beholder; people view and calibrate success in different ways. Those who recognize these different connections often develop the ability to motivate people to higher levels of performance, both by the way they define "success" and by how they instill pride along the way. Unfortunately, instilling pride in others is easier to do in some environments than in others.

I first uncovered the power of the "closed loop of emotional energy" in an obvious place: high-performing workforces at Southwest Airlines, Marriott, the U.S. Marine Corps, and Microsoft. Pride is a natural by-product of the successes of those organizations. It is fairly common for their managers and leaders to draw upon pride as an ongoing source of motivation; those feelings are easy to come by. Yet what about companies that have historically not been remarkably successful? Can pride precipitate higher performance in those environments as well?

Certainly, the answer is yes—but it happens less frequently and is more difficult than in the perennial achievers. Not surprisingly, therefore, prospective "pride-builders" can usually learn more about how to instill the pride that leads to higher performance from the proven pride-builders in more traditional environments than from those in peak-performing environments. The difference, of course, is that in companies that experience perennial successes, pride follows naturally; in other organizations, pride-builders have to apply their ingenuity to instill pride during periods of low or sporadic business success.

PRIDE GENERATES HIGHER PERFORMANCE

We know that pride is a primary source of energy and emotional commitment in enterprises that consistently outperform their competition.[1] While it is less obvious perhaps, we find clear evidence in traditional large companies that those managers who excel at instilling pride in their workers also deliver higher levels of both economic and market performance over time than their peers. For example, we asked the Manufacturing Managers Council at General Motors to identify twenty of the best "pride-builders" in GM's North American Manufacturing organization. Our case studies of these plant managers confirmed their reliance on pride as a primary source of motivation (described in more detail in chapter 6).

General Motors regularly measures its plants on five

1. See *Peak Performance: Aligning the Hearts and Minds of Your Employees* (Cambridge, MA: Harvard University Press, 2000).

basic elements of performance: safety, people satisfaction, product quality, responsiveness to customers, and cost. When we compared the performance of the twenty plants of those managers along each of these important metrics, their results consistently exceeded that of their peers. Specifically, the pride-builders outscored other plants on an index comparison by 83 to 65 on safety, 79 to 69 on people satisfaction, 53 to 47 on quality, and 69 to 65 on cost. Only on responsiveness did the pride-builder index fall short, and that was caused by a model changeover at one plant plus the start-up of another during this period.

While it is always difficult to separate the "chicken and egg" aspects of performance results and feelings of pride, the best motivators believe that instilling pride is what enables them to get higher levels of performance from their people. Of the over fifty pride-builders we have studied during the last two years, all deliver superior performance results for their enterprise—and all attribute their success to an ability to instill pride among their people *before the fact, i.e., before business success is assured and final results can be determined.*

A BROAD SPECTRUM

Human motivation is a moving target. Since everyone's personal circumstances change over time, we are motivated by different things at different stages in our life. We each define success in different ways and take pride in doing different things well. As a result, the sources of pride that motivate us cover a fairly broad spectrum, some of which produce "good" results for the enterprises we work for and some of which produce "bad" results. In describing this spectrum, it is useful to categorize the sources of pride into two basic groups: self-serving and institution-building. Clearly, neither category is completely good or bad in terms of results for the enterprise. For example, self-serving pride can motivate a person to work hard to keep her job, earn more money, and influence more people to help her. These motivations are typically good for the enterprise. However, self-serving pride can also motivate people to pursue money and material possessions as well as power and position above all else. When these motives lead to the exploitation of others for personal gain, the enterprise suffers.

Similarly, institution-building pride can motivate people behaviors that are bad for the enterprise. For example, an overemphasis on individual skill development and "teaming" can cause people to take pride in goals that supersede company priorities, create "marketable résumé" profiles, and pursue undisciplined teaming efforts in ways that are costly and confusing. Good results accrue to the enterprise only when the emphasis is on individual and group efforts that fit with organizational priorities and enhance long-term business success. The best leaders and managers will influence people to take pride in achieving personal goals that align with company goals, building skills that match company needs, and creating teams that achieve important business results. Institution-building pride typically favors the long-term success of an enterprise more than self-serving pride. Nonetheless, the challenge for any leadership system is to integrate sources of pride that will optimize the "good" motivational results and minimize "bad" motivational results—simply stated, to make sure that institution-building pride counterbalances self-serving pride.

Moreover, the forces that motivate us tend to shift depending on our personal needs as well as where we stand in the organizational hierarchy. Abraham Maslow's classic hierarchy of needs remains hard to dispute; the basic need for food and physical protection comes first. If you are stranded on a desert island like Robinson Crusoe or Tom Hanks in the movie *Castaway*, you are motivated by the need to survive until you can be rescued.

Beyond the survival imperative, however, we are motivated to provide safety and comfort for ourselves and our family. Only then, as Maslow clarified, do we seek fulfillment as individuals and as members of societal groups. Ultimately, we want to both "stand out as an individual" as well as "be part of groups we respect"—but these are secondary motivators as long as survival, safety, and comfort are at issue. While seldom finite, our creature comfort needs can usually be defined in monetary terms, although everyone seeks a different level of comfort. And when comfort is replaced by luxury on the need scale, wealth creation becomes a primary motivator.

After all, accumulating wealth "beyond basic need" is perhaps one of the great entrepreneurial pastimes. The Horatio Alger dream is alive and well. Every person is assumed to be free to earn whatever he or she can. Since promotions are invariably calibrated in monetary terms, the more your job pays, the more important you feel. The harder you work, the more money you expect to earn, and the more material possessions you can accumulate. The more you accumulate, the more attention you can expect to attract from friends, neighbors, and colleagues. This kind of expectation is motivating for many people. As a result, it is hardly surprising that Americans are working longer than ever before and probably put in more on-the-job hours than people in any other industrial society.

Money is the way to accumulate possessions that enable us to rise on the scoreboard of comparative achievement. "Keeping up with the Joneses" motivates many people. A more sensible motivation is that of working hard now to avoid having to work later in life. Moving up Maslow's hierarchy of needs is a natural human proposition—and money is the basic enabler. Thus, focusing on earning more money is a natural incentive that is widely employed by organizations that can afford it. However, it is seldom as powerful or lasting a motivator as intrinsic or institution-building pride. Those feelings generated by earnings can have a hollow ring if people do not admire us for other reasons.

These other reasons reflect other human needs that are simply not well defined by monetary wealth. They are the intrinsic or humanistic needs that spur people to try for their "personal best" or to seek their full potential, to be associated with colleagues they admire and respect, and to contribute to the well-being of others. Striving to meet these needs produces feelings of pride that are motivating—and usually completely independent of whatever monetary value society might establish. Whatever makes people feel proud of their efforts invariably explains their motivation to excel. Most of us work hardest at those tasks that make us feel proud based upon our personal values or beliefs. For some people, the amount of money they earn is the best way to evaluate how they are doing relative to others. For others, their recognized role in business and society is the best way. Many people, however, labor in ways that are not particularly lucrative or easily recognizable by title or position. They must rely on whatever reinforces feelings of intrinsic pride in what they do, how they do it, with and for whom they do it, and what it means to others whom they respect. For motivational purposes, it is useful to differentiate between self-serving and institution-building pride.

SELF-SERVING PRIDE

This kind of pride encompasses both power and materialism, and the latter is primarily a game of "show me the money"—and the more you can earn, accumulate, and visibly deploy, the better. People who play this game well focus their attention on whatever will reward them the most monetarily, and whatever will position them to control the most resources (human and economic). Hence, they are likely to shift their allegiances to whatever organizations or occupational pursuits offer the highest monetary compensation, promise the greatest wealth-accumulation opportunities, and thereby provide the most personal recognition and influence. Not surprisingly, these people are usually the first to leave an organization or occupation when economic returns start to falter. Loyalty and commitment play secondary roles in their motivation.

The disturbing collapse of Enron in 2001 provided a glaring example of how the unrelenting pursuit of monetary gain and personal power can lead intelligent executives astray and quickly erode institutional balance. *Fortune* magazine called it a "debacle of arrogance and greed." The Enron story, of course, is much more complex than that phrase would suggest, and many factors were involved in the company's downfall. From a motivational point of view, however, two important lessons emerge from the Enron story: (1) the pursuit of financial gain as the primary motivator promotes arrogant behavior and unwarranted risk-taking, and (2) that pursuit leads to an overreliance on individual achievement and personal power that rarely sustains enterprise-wide performance over time.

But Enron is an extreme example of self-serving pride out of control. Let's consider the less extreme case of Anil Xavier (disguised name), who was employed by BMC, an early contender in the software business in Texas. When I interviewed Anil for research on my previous book, *Peak Performance,* he was a highly regarded software designer for BMC. The key to their early success could be found in two segments of their workforce: the senior account sales representatives (some of whom made more money than the CEO) and the "product authors" or software designers. These two groups were highly motivated examples of entrepreneurialism in action: employees engaged in high-risk, high-reward challenges that offered the promise of personal financial independence.

Anil was proud that he earned more than $1 million annually, owned a Jaguar convertible, and could easily afford to charter a private plane to take his family on annual ski vacations at Vail. During the interview, he focused his remarks strictly on the commercial results of his products, i.e., the economic return. Little mention was made of the quality of his design work, the caliber of his colleagues, or the reactions of his customers beyond their willingness to pay high prices. Anil is no longer with BMC, having left the company for a better-paying opportunity when his bonus was reduced shortly after BMC encountered an economic downturn. Like most people who thrive on materialistic pride, he was quick to move on to a higher bidder and showed little commitment to riding out the downturn with BMC.

There is little question that high levels of individual achievement are motivated by ego as well as self-serving pride. And in some situations, such as individual sports or artistic pursuits, such motivations are both powerful and appropriate. During 2001 and 2002, Jennifer Capriati was rated the top female tennis player in the world. She had to work hard to reach that level, coming back from her disappointing early years on the professional tennis tour. She was also highly motivated to stay at that level and takes great pride in getting to and being at the top of her chosen profession. An article in the June 2, 2002, issue of the *New York Times* describes this challenge:

> At times, the strain on Capriati has been visible. She has yelled expletives at umpires and complained about fans. To some tennis officials, Capriati has appeared fragile in her desire to make her moment last as long as possible. Privately, those officials feel the pressure led to the profane tirade she directed at Billie Jean King last month. After King dismissed her from the Fed Cup team for her refusal to conform to team practice rules, Capriati lashed out at the captain and caretaker of the women's tour. With the French Open looming, Capriati felt her practice routine superseded team rules.
>
> Structure and simplicity have been the foundation of Capriati's return. Even for Fed Cup, Capriati was not about to change her approach to tennis. It was an act of selfishness on Capriati's part, but so be it. With that backdrop, it was not surprising when Capriati agreed with a recent comment from John McEnroe concerning the self-centered nature and ego top [tennis] players need to drive them to the top and keep them there.
>
> "I think ego is pride," Capriati said. "To get to the top,

you have to have a lot of pride. That's not giving up. At the Australian Open for me this year, that was pride and ego and I didn't want to lose. If you don't have that, you're not a champion, you're not a fighter. . . . I would have to say you have to be a little bit selfish just because there's so much that requires being done."[2]

For the most part, professional tennis is an individual sport. Hence, self-serving pride is the primary motivational force. When a team aspect of the sport (e.g., the Fed Cup) comes into play, however, there is also a real need for institution-building pride to take over; otherwise the team will come apart. The same holds true for business enterprises. Unless self-serving pride is wisely counterbalanced by institution-building pride, the performance of the enterprise will suffer.

INSTITUTION-BUILDING PRIDE

In marked contrast, institution-building or intrinsic pride feeds on character and emotional commitment that tends to further collective rather than strictly individual sets of interests. Since a monetary scoreboard is less relevant here, people focus on the more basic performance factors of customer satisfaction, peer and mentor approval, capability development, and quality of work products. Institution-building pride fosters inner feelings of fundamental self-worth, respected group association, and personal development satisfaction.

Importantly, self-discipline is a fundamental attribute of people who are motivated by institution-building pride. They

2. "Capriati Protecting Her Revival," *New York Times*, June 2, 2002.

focus on the disciplined behaviors that directly affect the last-ing determinants of enterprise success. The U.S. Marine Corps provides one of the best examples of the motivational power of self-discipline and the lasting impact of institution-building pride.

For over two hundred years now the Marines have been winning critical battles for the United States and its allies. Since the Marines are not "at war" most of the time, the task of motivating the troops to be "always prepared for battle" is no small challenge. And the Corps does it by instilling pride that comes more from self-discipline than from command-and-control discipline.

Marine recruits are often people whom most companies never recruit, e.g., high-school and college dropouts and those who are unemployed and/or are from broken homes. Most of them join the Marines without a set of strong per-sonal values to guide their behavior and with little exposure to discipline of any kind. At Parris Island, South Carolina, where new recruits become Marines, the transition starts with strongly enforced, top-down discipline embodied by role-model drill instructors. The basic program consists of twelve weeks dedicated almost entirely to inculcating the USMC values of honor, courage, and commitment. However, by the end of basic training the top-down forces have sys-tematically been superseded by the more subtle and powerful peer discipline and self-discipline. When self-discipline "kicks in," pride takes over because the recruits discover they are capable of achieving and contributing much more than they ever dreamed possible. Imagine the pride they feel as they conquer their instinctive fear of heights by leaping off forty-foot platforms with only a rope to slow their fall; or conquer other physical obstacles they would heretofore not even attempt; or, most important, earn the respect of the DI role models who initially terrified and intimidated them. Intrinsic pride based upon self-discipline, role models, and values is the primary source of motivation in the Corps. And strong emotional commitment is at the heart of a Marine's motivation.

My visits to Quantico, Camp Lejeune, and Parris Island were replete with examples of how institution-building pride is instilled to motivate frontline Marines. To cite a few:

- Wick Murray, my first guide and sponsor at Quantico, reminded me of how Marine units take great pride in bringing back more of their dead and wounded survivors from common battlegrounds than any other armed service. A private first class aide to General Keith Holcomb made the unsolicited proud observation to me, "I know the general would never leave me behind in battle—nor would I ever leave him behind."

- I watched the recruits struggle to swim in full battle dress and then beam with pride when they made it across a fifty-foot pool for the first time. It brought forth the permanent mental picture I have of the face of my five-year-old after finishing his first short bike ride without crashing into the bushes. If you don't think that first-time five-year-old bike riders and first-time Marine swimmers are both highly motivated to extend their distances on the next try, you are badly mistaken.

- At the Leadership Recognition Course for officer candidates at Quantico, Virginia, a series of physical "puzzles" or problems are set up for four-person groups of candidates to solve. For example, one problem requires the group to figure out how to get a two-hundred-pound dummy (surrogate for a "wounded Marine") across a wading pool without touching the water, utilizing only a set of four planks of varying lengths. These puzzles are not designed to be "solved" in the time allotted because their purpose is to teach leadership options. However, every now and then a group does succeed, and when that happens, the expressions of pride look a lot like the facial expressions of my five-year-old bike rider.

- The final event at Parris Island boot camp carries the ominous label The Crucible (formerly called Warrior Week). It consists of roughly fifty-four hours of uninterrupted physically and mentally stressing activities with little food and sleep. Each of the sixteen different exercises begins at what is called a Warrior Station, which is marked with a plaque and description of a frontline hero (usually a Medal of Honor winner) in a wartime event similar to what the group is about to experience. These true-life stories evoke feelings of pride in the Marine heritage, as well as anticipatory feelings of pride for what the recruits are about to accomplish. The most moving aspect of The Crucible, however, comes at the end of the fifty-four-hour ordeal. Each recruit receives his "globe, anchor, and eagle" pin (the official Marine Corps emblem) from his drill instructor, who has also been through all sixteen simulated battle "ordeals" with his recruits. As the emblem is pinned on, there is seldom a dry eye on either side as both DI and recruit savor the feelings of pride in their joint accomplishment. Memories of this event remain sources of pride that motivate value-based behaviors throughout the military and civilian lives of the new Marines ("once a Marine, always a Marine" is no idle shibboleth).

Institution-building pride is based upon largely intangible values and basic human emotions, rather than tangible compensation and crystal-clear logic. The real strength of this kind of pride as a motivator, however, is that it works across the broad base of organizations like the Marines, where money is not a realistic source of motivation. Most large enterprises, unfortunately, employ thousands of workers who work within compensation bands that offer little monetary incentive. Simply stated, what the company can afford to offer in worker compensation is limited, and advancement opportunities narrow quickly. Fortunately for such companies, while money may attract and retain people, it is rarely at the heart of what motivates them to excel except perhaps at the highest levels of an organization.

Both Southwest Airlines and The Home Depot are excellent examples of companies that can use "wealth accumulation opportunity" to attract and retain people, since they have been successful growth organizations that the stock market has valued highly over time. Clearly, stock ownership means something in both enterprises. Yet it is clear from our research that people within both of those workforces are much more motivated by intrinsic rather than materialistic pride. For example, the institution-building pride at Southwest Airlines comes from tangible results for the enterprise: (1) five years of leading the industry in customer-service performance metrics, and (2) an airplane turnaround time (the time from touchdown to takeoff) that is about half of what any other carrier can claim, i.e., eighteen minutes for SWA versus over thirty minutes for most competitors. Southwest employees know they are the best and are highly motivated to continue that legacy.

At The Home Depot, employees take great pride in

"seeing smiles on the faces" of satisfied customers. During an interview with a store manager in Atlanta, I asked how he knows that his level of customer service is higher than what the customers experience at the Lowes competitive outlet across the street. His answer was by "counting the smiling faces" leaving both stores. But, of course, customer service at Home Depot is tracked much more seriously than by simply counting smiley faces. Managers walk the talk, interview customers in the store, probe into every complaint, and pay close attention to what the competition is doing.

Compare the story of Deb Burke, then in her fifth year at The Home Depot, with that of Anil Xavier at BMC.[3] Her husband is a successful businessman in his own right, so Deb was looking for interesting work rather than money. With absolutely no relevant experience, her first assignment was in the millwork department of one of Home Depot's Atlanta stores. Millwork is purchased primarily by professional carpenters, craftsmen, and building contractors, so her early attempts to please her customers were no small challenge. Rough-hewn builders have little patience for naive responses to their questions, so Deb had to learn millwork in a hurry. She took great pride in both mastering her complex product line and developing a unique ability to use her instinctive customer-service skills to remind a disgruntled, complaining customer that "Look, I'm just a *mom!*"—which invariably turned the complainer into an apologetic helper. Deb's husband asked her every payday, somewhat facetiously, "Did you pick up your check today, or are you still working just for the fun of it?" By and large, Deb really did work more "for fun" than for money, since her motivation and pride

3. See *Peak Performance.*

came from millwork mastery and tough-customer approval; money plays no role in that equation. When last we checked, Deb was still working hard at The Home Depot, taking pride in her product knowledge, customer skills, and colleagues— and paying little or no attention to her paycheck. Intrinsic pride works that way.

DIFFERENT EARLY EXPERIENCES INFLUENCE MOTIVATION

Self-serving pride is not as satisfying—and not as motivating—as the intrinsic, institution-building pride we feel when others admire us for the fundamentals, namely:

- Our work product and what it does for others.
- The skills we have mastered to obtain our work position or role.
- The people who respect us for what we do rather than how much we earn.
- The reputation our enterprise or work group has earned over time.
- The people (customers, colleagues, agents) who are attracted to what we do.
- The accomplishments of others that can legitimately be attributed to our support or sponsorship.

These fundamentals are the sources of institution-building pride. Their relative importance to anyone, however, is a function of who and what has influenced that person in the past as well as what influences them currently. As a result, employees differ in what will motivate them, and the better employers will recognize that by the range of tools and mechanisms they use to instill pride. Our relatives and schoolmates from childhood have a major and often lasting influence on what we take pride in today. And those influences are sometimes more significant than what organizational role models or employers say or do. The ways in which very different early influences can produce similar sets of motivations and sources of intrinsic pride can be seen in the following two leaders in the General Motors family—one who came up through the management ranks, and one who was a product of the United Automobile Workers (UAW) union.

Tom Weekley of the UAW and Jay Wilber of General Motors Corporation are both highly motivated, upper-level managers within the UAW-GM Quality Network.[4] In fact, they are "zealots" with respect to their roles in shaping and leading the Quality Network. This impressive organization struggles to imbue thousands of North American workers across three different institutions (United Auto Workers, Delphi Automotive Systems, and General Motors) with the basic values and best practices of quality management. It is perhaps the most extensively designed and engineered quality management system in the world. Jay and Tom are relentless believers in this effort and, even after ten years, still spend every waking hour thinking about how to "do it better." While General Motors and the UAW pay Jay and Tom well,

---

4. Tom Weekley was reassigned to the UAW-GM Center for Human Resources—Health and Safety. He was replaced by Tom Walsh, UAW assistant director, an equally committed and dedicated UAW leader, who has also been associated with the UAW-GM Quality Network since 1990.

it is not the money that motivates this kind of emotional commitment. Interestingly, these two individuals came from very different backgrounds with very different influences that explain their motivations.

Jay's family history is embedded with General Motors' managerial tradition. His father and his grandfather worked together as supervisors in a GM plant in Flint, Michigan. He grew up with stories of the 1937 strikes—"how men who worked for them prior to the sit-down became embittered and angry in their quest for changes in the workplace and their struggles to begin a union to represent them with management."

Jay himself was hired in June of 1965 as a fourth-generation family member (his great-grandfather had been an hourly assembler for Fisher Body). Working his way up through a number of union jobs, he was promoted to process engineer in April 1969 and thus became a member of management. The next year, at age twenty-three, he was promoted to supervisor, skilled trades. That day his father also gave him a folded piece of paper from his wallet (which he had received from Jay's grandfather) that contained the following poem of unidentified origin:

Don't Quit

When things go wrong, as they sometimes will,
When the road you're trudging seems all uphill,
When the funds are low, and the debts are high
And you want to smile, but you have to sigh,
When care is pressing you down a bit,
Rest if you must, but don't quit.

Life is queer with its twists and turns,
As every one of us sometimes learns,
And many a failure turns about,
When he might have won had he stuck it out;
Don't give up though the pace seems slow
You may succeed with another blow.
Success is failure turned inside out,
The silver tint of the clouds of doubt,
And you never can tell how close you are
It may be near when it seems so far.
So stick to the fight when you're hardest hit,
It's when things seem worse,
That you must not quit.

—Author unknown

These are the values that have guided Jay's working life—and they define the most important sources of his pride. It was pretty simple, therefore, for GM to connect with and benefit from that pride in motivating Jay's efforts over the last thirty-plus years.

Tom Weekley came from a very different background. His personal beliefs and values were influenced by a vast array of experiences, mostly union-based. He began his GM career on March 7, 1970, at the new General Motors fabricating plant in Lordstown, Ohio, following several years as a member of the long-established union at Chrysler. Since the Lordstown plant was new, the union was not yet recognized as the bargaining agent for employees at the plant. Tom encountered many unpleasant situations because of this gap, and he soon came to believe deeply in the need for workers to have input into their jobs, as well as for management to listen to what they had to say. The situation soon led Tom to seek out the union organizer, although he had no intention of being involved in the union. Nonetheless, he was elected committee person by his fellow workers at the age of twenty-two. Tom lived through numerous unpleasant incidents and management confrontations at Lordstown. In fact, he was eventually suspended and fired from General Motors several times for actively protecting the interests of workers.

Just as this downward cycle of dysfunctional relationships was gaining momentum, Tom had the good fortune to begin working with a labor supervisor named Bill Malone. He single-handedly turned the relationship in Tom's plant completely around from one of antagonism to one of cooperation and concern for both workers and the corporation. Malone's secret was simple—always stand up for what is right rather than what is expedient. In Tom's words, Bill clearly demonstrated how the values and integrity of "one man can make a radical difference in a situation that seems impossible." Previously, Tom's focus had been on winning battles for the union rather than finding ways to integrate the valid interests of two different constituencies. Bill demonstrated through his attitude and actions (versus words and debates) that winning for the union was not as good as getting what is right for building the institution, including both workforce and corporate interests. Under Bill and Tom, this approach completely changed relationships at this plant, where labor peace continues to produce increasing levels of performance.

Thus began Tom's belief in and emotional commitment to doing the right thing rather than the expedient one—which became the source of his pride and emotional commitment to the Quality Network, where he and Jay Wilber first came together as a result of separate assignments by the UAW and GM. For years thereafter, Tom worked alongside Jay to forge an "impossible partnership" based on finding the common ground. There is little doubt of the parallelism and power of Jay's and Tom's pride and emotional commitment to GM's performance—even though one comes from a managerial heritage and the other from the heart of unionism.

Tom and Jay take great pride in their respective and joint roles (which they would describe as modest) in one of the most famous union/management agreements in General Motors' history: the Toledo Accord. In February of 1987, the culmination of the continuing joint improvement efforts of General Motors and UAW leaders occurred at a quality-strategy conference in Toledo, Ohio. This simple, signed statement of agreement was the goal and vision that Tom and Jay had devoted over ten years of their working life to making a reality. The Toledo Accord remains a source of great pride to General Motors and UAW people alike, and it continues to be a source of motivational energy for thousands who are directly involved in making the Toledo Accord a permanent leadership and behavioral policy. The opening paragraph of this accord (personally signed by fifteen top leaders of GM and the UAW) speaks for itself, and it helps to define the source of Tom's and Jay's commitment to—and pride in—their respective roles in quality performance at GM:

> The undersigned leadership of General Motors and the UAW is jointly committed to securing General Motors' position in the market and the job security of its employees in every phase of the corporation through an ongoing process of producing the highest quality customer valued products. The parties agree that the production of world-class quality products is the key to our survival and jointly commit to pursue the implementation of [a] jointly developed quality strategy.

Tom and Jay have come to appreciate the motives of the other and to convert those different motives to a powerful "common ground." It would be hard to find a stronger supporter of union priorities among the leadership ranks of GM or Delphi than Jay Wilber. And it would be equally hard to find a better interpreter of the management priorities of GM and Delphi within the extensive UAW union leadership system than Tom Weekley. Perhaps they influence each other now as much as anything else does.[5]

Like Tom and Jay, most of us want to take pride in what we do and with whom we do it. We all take pride in different things, and we all draw on different legacies and people who have influenced us. When all is said and done, however, it is the pride we feel, be it self-serving or institution-building, that spurs us on to excel.

---

5. The descriptions in this chapter about Jay C. Wilber and Thomas L. Weekley were excerpted with their permission from their book, *United We Stand*, published in 1996 by McGraw-Hill.

CHAPTER 2

■

MONEY TALKS; MATERIALISTIC PRIDE LISTENS

■

I t almost goes without saying that the prospect of earning more money motivates higher performance. In fact, most well-intended managers believe that the best way to reward as well as motivate their employees is by dangling more "coin of the realm" in front of them. Yet this conventional wisdom of "pay for performance" is both incomplete and misleading. While employees pay attention to the promise of higher earnings, they are often more motivated emotionally by other things, particularly when their incremental earnings opportunity is relatively modest. Moreover, relying on money as the primary source of motivation can get expensive for the company, particularly if it doesn't really produce commensurate results. Nonetheless, "pay for performance" persists as the underlying premise of most formal compensation programs. And many leaders are convinced that the more closely pay is tied to performance, the better.

Designers of compensation programs are invariably striving to motivate people to work in ways that will not only earn the individual more money but will also deliver results that are good for the company. Well-designed compensation programs are also intended to motivate people to take a longer-term view of what they do and how they do it. But the main benefit of monetary compensation is its immediate measurability; it constitutes one of the most widely accepted ways to distinguish the top performers from the average. Hence, as long as we can be perfectly clear about what attitudes and actions will result in more money and wealth for both employees and employers and can design pay programs to reward those conditions, what's the problem? Who cares if people take more pride in the possessions that they can accumulate than they do in their work, as long as that work leads to enterprise leadership and success over time? Many companies base their entire motivational system on this kind of thinking. In situations where rational compliance by employees, i.e., following the rules and doing only what is "expected," allows the company to succeed, there is little need to seek emotional commitment. Emotional commitment, of course, is very different from simply doing what is expected. People who are emotionally committed to something—be it a person, a group, an enterprise, a cause, or an aspiration—behave in ways that defy logic and often produce results that are well beyond expectations. They pursue impossible dreams, work ridiculous hours, and resolve unsolvable problems. They even create the infamous "killer apps" (unbeatable product "inventions") that truly innovative enterprises such as Apple, Pfizer, and Hewlett-Packard have used to reshape entire industries.

A RISKY SOURCE OF MOTIVATION

The issue here is with the definition of performance. If you can define performance in terms that are easily measurable and that include all behaviors required for long-term enterprise success, money works. If not, money diverts.

For example, a few years ago I gave a talk to a large group of investment bankers and traders at J. P. Morgan Bank. The subject was team performance, and the group was interested in increasing their team performance capability to better serve their larger accounts. Seeking team performance among the high individual earners from the trading and investment banking disciplines, however, is not a task for the faint at heart. Since they are strongly motivated by high earnings possibilities, you can rest assured that any notion of moderating any individual's pay in the interest of the more illusive possibility of team earnings is not well received. It is not exactly a culture of greed, but it is certainly one of "show me the money." One of the senior women in the audience named Marjorie asked me a pointed question: "Mr. Katzenbach, do you really think we can get our high-paid people to even consider the discipline you advocate for performing teams when their compensation is so heavily weighted by their individual deals?" The answer, of course, was frustrating to both Marjorie and me: "Probably not, unless you can somehow nullify the powerful monetary incentive to score on the big deals."

Unfortunately, this problem plagues any company, regardless of industry, that bases its formal compensation on emphasizing significant distinctions between levels of individual performance. Paying a lot of money to individual performers virtually precludes the behaviors required for team performance. Moreover, my friend and coauthor of *The Wisdom of Teams,* Douglas K. Smith, argues persuasively that there are few, if any, effective team incentive pay programs simply because all formal pay programs presume individual scoring and advancement—a concept that strongly inhibits team performance. The good news, of course, is that performing teams can and do motivate themselves primarily by instilling pride in their collective performance—completely independent of the individual compensation of the members. Monetary compensation is simply not a motivational factor within a true performing team because the extra performance the group achieves results from collective or joint efforts that are rarely recognized by monetary rewards.

Most people in business today pursue a lifestyle that benefits from earning more money. We also want our children to have a better life than we had. My parents, as I suspect did many of yours, both worked in multiple jobs for well over thirty years, primarily to send me through college and graduate school. They also urged me to "major in business so you can afford a better life than ours." Probably without meaning to, they were sewing the seeds of materialism into my motivation.

Unfortunately, McKinsey continued, probably unintentionally, to cultivate those seeds. At first, money was not the issue, although I was certainly proud of my $9,600 annual starting compensation. But once on board as a McKinsey associate, my efforts were motivated by the prospect of group approval of people I admired and respected. Soon client approval became an integral part my motivation as well. And pride in the approval of my colleagues and clients soon caused me to forget completely about the money. Midway through my career, however, money reared its ugly head again. The Firm's partner evaluation processes (which were world-class, in my view) were based on a balanced set of criteria that included fact-based assessments of my relative value to clients, contributions to the firm, and development of the people who worked with me. That's the good news. The bad news is that while the evaluation process rigorously looked at those three primary criteria, it also ranked people accordingly and used monetary reward as its primary "score-keeping" mechanism. As long as the amount of my compensation was not extreme, and the compensation gap between my peers and me remained reasonably narrow and explainable, pride in group approval remained a strong, primary motivator.

To some extent, my motivation changed during my later years as a partner of the Firm. Starting in the mid-1980s, McKinsey's success enabled them to increase individual compensation significantly, as well as the spread of compensation one might earn for different levels of performance. Increasingly, therefore, some of the more ambitious members of the partnership began to focus more attention on the monetary rewards. Starting from pay levels that were probably closer to that of the accounting profession, high-performing partners could envision earning as much as leading investment bankers, lawyers, and many CEOs. As a result, money threatened to become a more central element in my motivation—and was accompanied by an increasing interest in materialistic gains. Like most partners, I wanted to be ranked highly by the partnership evaluation system, which is one of the more fact-based and fair systems in the world.

During this period, Marvin Bower frequently reminded us about the dangers of self-serving materialistic motivations. While such motivations may start innocently enough, they can easily get out of hand. At the extreme, they evolve into greed, vanity, and the subordination of the values and institution-building sources of pride that were the intended foundation of the overall reward system.

From McKinsey's point of view, however, the motivations remained in balance. The strength and pervasiveness of

McKinsey's value system remained a powerful counterbalance that provided an effective warning against the materialistic quicksand trap—particularly at the partner level, where the values of superior client service and partnership prevailed. Many McKinsey associates, however, were more motivated by individual achievement and personal growth opportunities and could easily envision alternative job opportunities. Institution-building values did not have nearly the influence in their motivation that you find at the partner level.

To oversimplify, McKinsey associate behaviors were more influenced by a strong motivation to become a partner as fast as possible or to leave to pursue a different career—in large part to enhance their lifestyle. And as the system increased the relative compensation and the spread, it reinforced that source of pride and motivation. Therefore, it should have been no surprise when many presumably committed associates left the firm in pursuit of the gold mine at the end of the e-commerce rainbow. Pride in values and professional achievement was being inadvertently superseded by the prospects of pride in wealth and financial independence. It was a signal to many McKinsey leaders that self-serving sources of pride (financial reward and materialistic pride) were beginning to encroach on the more lasting sources of institution-building pride (values and group accomplishment).

ADVANTAGES OF SELF-SERVING PRIDE

Despite the institution-building drawbacks of monetary rewards, the logic behind relying on them remains reasonably compelling:

1. *Self-serving pride is unavoidable* because it stems from basic human needs. We must have money to buy the food, clothing, and shelter that our families need to survive. This motivation transcends different nationalities. In most areas of Western civilization, these basic needs naturally evolve into strong desires for more tasty food, more attractive clothing, and more comfortable shelters. People want to be admired by others for what they have accomplished, and that easily translates into a desire to own more. A person's perceived self-importance can be enhanced by simply owning luxuries well beyond any definition of the basic necessities of life. In some ways, this helps explain why self-serving pride can readily influence behaviors that have little do with basic necessities. It feeds into habits that seem to say material possessions reflect all accomplishments and sources of pride. Although I believe it is incomplete as a motivational system, it is not all bad.

2. *Monetary awards are "scorecards of accomplishment"* because everyone understands the scale. Material possessions serve as indicators of talent and achievement. Some wealthy people who make noble and commendable distributions of their monetary wealth are still motivated by the size of that wealth as a scorecard of their accomplishments. In fact, wise leaders of nonprofit

institutions (e.g., universities, hospitals, and artistic organizations) nourish and cultivate the motivation of the rich to have their names forever emblazoned on the objects of their generosity such as buildings and research centers. The lists of donors to great universities such as Harvard or Stanford are published, if not ranked monetarily, for all to see. A few months ago, I attended a performance of the Dance Theatre of Harlem at the Charleston Spoleto arts festival, which is an excellent community service effort that brings talented art and entertainment groups into the city. The festival is successful and relies on private donations to sustain it. A couple in front of me were entirely focused on the donations list in the program to see who was in what donation category. I overhead one of them mention the need to elevate their contribution next year to get into a higher category. Clearly, it is human nature to want to be admired for our good works, and if that serves to motivate more people of means to fund good works, society clearly benefits.

3. *Money is a clear way to separate the performers from the nonperformers* because it is easily tracked and compared. Even at lower levels in organizations, workers take pride in both earnings and possessions as indicators of their accomplishments relative to others. Union workers are understandably proud of the boats they own, the vacations they can afford, and the neighborhoods where they live. And they are certainly motivated to upgrade those affordables. The entire union movement is intended to ensure that workers are treated with respect by employers and that they receive a fair day's

pay for a fair day's work. In addition, most employees in the business world seek some kind of visible score-card to remind them and others of their accomplishments and how they are doing relative to others. The beauty of tangible, visible possessions is that they tend to speak for themselves in this regard.

Employees typically assume that people who earn more money and acquire more material possessions are the better performers. And they resent it when they see poor performers being disproportionately rewarded. Thus, success and money tend to become indistinguishable in our minds.

4. *The monetary value of a job helps candidates determine where they want to work* because higher compensation suggests a better job. Money differentials make it easy for the more versatile job seekers to decide which organizational units and positions to favor. While not entirely a matter of "show me the money," it comes close. Employees who are motivated by materialism are easily attracted to the highest bidder. In an enterprise where employee mobility is critical, monetary incentives can be helpful. How often have we envied a colleague who was offered a higher-paying job in another department? The now nearly universal practice of internal job posting makes it much easier for any employee to determine where she can expect to earn the most money. The bad news is that an executive or manager can be confident of keeping her best people only if she continues to pay them the highest amount of money.

For many business leaders, these advantages of self-serving pride are good enough. They are tangible, acceptable, effective, and readily understandable. Compensation pro-grams and monetary incentives that are well designed and well applied will certainly induce behaviors that management can control and align for the performance of the enterprise. Is there any reason to look further?

Absolutely. Some of the best-performing enterprises (to be discussed in chapter 5), particularly those that have sus-tained a higher level of workforce performance than their competitors for more than a decade, place much more emphasis on nonmonetary incentives. Monetary incentives that capitalize on self-serving pride have significant disad-vantages if an enterprise needs employees who are not con-tent with just meeting expectations to excel relative to the competition. Most important, in my opinion, if emotional commitment among critical segments of your workforce is necessary to sustain a competitive advantage, the pitfalls of self-serving pride far outweigh its advantages. If systems are robust, they are less sensitive to self-serving pride. However, if variation can occur in the system, then emotional commit-ment is key to sustainable competitiveness.

PITFALLS OF SELF-SERVING PRIDE

Like it or not, self-serving pride based on materialism and power is seldom an admirable attribute. Most people don't want to be accused of being materialistic or power-hungry and will typically find ways to cloak such motives in more admirable rationales. "We really need this [plush] office space to convince customer executives of the high quality of our company's services." Or "I am chartering a jet to Vail because I am too busy to use commercial options." Or "we really need a [larger] home in this [better] neighborhood so our children will have the chances we never had."

When the dotcom craziness hit the U.S. economy in the nineties, the impact of materialistic pride became crystal clear. Thousands of people in all walks of life jumped on the bandwagon—either by investing their hard-earned money in volatile stocks or by leaving traditional jobs with established companies for the lure of big money. Highly successful and respected companies such as General Electric, ExxonMobil, Motorola, and McKinsey, along with most of the financial services industry, lost young people in droves and were unable to attract comparable replacements. These people found it difficult to remain in more traditional cultures that seemed to be emphasizing earnings opportunities as a primary motivator but could not match the big-money promises of the dotcoms.

Clearly, money is a motivating force of significant proportions, and materialistic pride plays an important role in aligning the decisions and actions of lots of people. Nonetheless, when it comes to generating higher levels of performance over the long term, self-serving pride has many shortfalls, including the following:

1. *Money attracts and retains people better than it motivates them to excel.* Unquestionably, many people have been attracted to join companies like Microsoft, The Home Depot, Apple, and Southwest Airlines because of the opportunity to own stock that promised to grow dramatically in value over time. The initial motivational force, however, does not explain why so many employees at those institutions remain determined to excel with respect to serving customers, designing innovative prod-

ucts, and doing better than the competition. Focusing on those activities will not really earn them more spendable cash. While employees of these enterprises are interested in and proud of stock-value increases, few of them will have much direct influence on those increases, so stock value seldom motivates them to excel on the job. It is much more likely that "what turns them on" to high levels of job performance is the intrinsic pride they feel in "putting smiles on the customers' faces," "turning planes around in record time," or "making products that change the world."

2. *Money works only as long as you can pay more than the competition.* From an enterprise point of view, money only works as long as some other enterprise does not offer your top performers a higher amount. And as implied before, whenever the company faces tough times, the positive aspects of monetary incentives turn negative. The best people leave just when you need them the most. And the mediocre performers hang on as long as possible, because they fear they cannot find good-paying jobs elsewhere. As a result, your workforce quickly gravitates to the lowest possible denominator—acceptable mediocrity. Threats of job loss and layoffs as well as reduced bonuses take over as negative motivating forces—or perhaps more aptly, the intimidating factors. Intimidation is certainly a proven way to enforce compliance; it is completely ineffective, however, when it comes to energizing positive emotional commitment.

3. *A monetary focus can obscure the fundamentals because you cannot easily convert short-term earnings into lasting value.* At best, monetary incentives moti-

vate only a narrow set of behaviors, and usually they create a self-interest emphasis that is not in the best interests of the company. For example, Silicon Valley sales forces are notorious for their relentless determination to get orders in before the end of the fourth quarter, since that will affect their annual commissions as well as stock market valuations. In the "new economy," legitimate investments are delayed, if not reduced, to ensure that quarterly earnings targets are met. The results required for lasting business success are seldom best defined in the short term.

4. *Self-serving employees can take advantage of monetary incentive plans.* In my experience, almost any short-term compensation program can be manipulated by clever employees to their advantage. If higher quarterly sales are what you pay for, you may find that you will get it at the expense of service, investment, and fair play. The smart salesperson can get his orders booked to his personal advantage. If a different product emphasis is what you pay for, it can often be achieved in the short term by not giving the customer what he really wants or needs.

5. *Money and title differentials work better at the top than at the bottom because the value-added differences are more evident.* Upper-level leaders and top executives are conditioned to pay more attention to things like earnings per share, return on capital, and wealth accumulation programs. For one thing, they understand the connections between those sophisticated indicators of enterprise success and their own performance. And, more important, most corporations make a point of paying

them for their specific contributions to such indicators. Last, but not least, there is usually room for a wider range of monetary and ego-satisfying rewards at the top levels of the corporation. Thus, we can easily recognize performance variations with pay and position differentials that are motivating. To put it bluntly, you cannot expect to motivate the broad base of employees with the same philosophy, approach, and tools that work at the top. The earnings, advancement, and wealth accumulation opportunities are completely different. And sometimes the fundamental values are different as well. Integrity at that top may mean always doing what is right for the company; at the front line it may mean always standing by your colleagues' right to have a job.

6. *Money and ego motivate individuals better than they do teams or groups.* Compensation systems are understandably and necessarily designed to reward individual performance. The better-performing individuals can expect to be around for years rather than months, and they can expect to advance into positions that pay them more. Hence, they can easily apply the monetary rewards of their labors to material possessions that improve their lifestyles and those of their families. Few of these conditions are true for teams or groups. Teams can seldom be compensated as a unit. Most teams are not expected to persist over time, and there is no simple way for such groups to advance as a group through normal organizational hierarchies to higher-paying opportunities.

7. *Materialism easily turns into greed and self-serving behaviors.* Perhaps the worst aspect of relying on

money as a primary motivator is the high risk of greed and self-serving motives taking over. It is a subtle transition and therefore seldom viewed as a danger by those who favor the directness and simplicity of money as a motivator. Yet even great institutions such as McKinsey and Goldman Sachs have seen the professional behaviors of their partners affected by greed. Fortunately, the strength of those firms' values seems to keep that danger to a few isolated cases—usually resulting in their separation from the firm. Other high-paying enterprises, however, have been less successful—particularly in the fast-paced and high-priced world of investment banking. A recent example in the business press highlighted the problem when a powerful partner with Credit Suisse made several different moves among top-notch investment banking houses in the last few years. Clearly, he is an extremely successful dealmaker with a cadre of capable talent surrounding him. It is also clear that whenever his individual earnings and freedom have been threatened, he moves on to another home.

MONEY HAS MOTIVATIONAL LIMITS

At the other end of the spectrum, realistic earnings expectations rather than greed are the problem. Consider the case of Eddie and Jennifer Bartholomew (names disguised). Eddie is a salesman for Alliant, a U.S. national food distribution company, whose motivational system for its sales force is based almost entirely on monetary incentives. Eddie is a classic example of an individual who is no longer motivated to work harder or smarter to earn more money, simply because his preferred lifestyle does not require it—nor is his earnings potential really high enough to get him to a much grander lifestyle. His wife, Jennifer, provides an interesting contrast of someone whose motivation is provided entirely by the nonmonetary aspects of her job. She works in an environment where pride-building skills predominate; Eddie works in an environment where such skills are in short supply.

Eddie is thirty-eight years old, married for twelve years to Jennifer, and the couple have three children plus a disabled parent to support. Three years ago, Eddie was recruited by Alliant for his current job from Sysco, a competitor, on the promise of a better territory, since the salary and commission scales of the two companies are similar. That promise never materialized, so Eddie earns about what he was earning before. Alliant regards Eddie as a good salesman, although he is not one of their top performers. The company places great emphasis on sales quotas and offers special bonuses to those who exceed those quotas. Many of their managers and executives also implicitly "threaten" the sales force with loss of jobs if quotas are not met. Food distribution is a tough business, and sales force turnover is high. Obviously, threats work best when other job alternatives are in short supply.

Recently, a new director of sales designed a different commission and bonus system to place greater weight on the more profitable product lines for Alliant. While Eddie's behavior shifted a bit as a result of that change, his monthly and annual earnings didn't change much. In fact, increasing his pay appreciably would require Eddie to work over sixty hours per week, thus eliminating precious weekend time with his children and aging father. Neither Eddie nor Jennifer wants him to make this trade-off. Consequently, Jennifer works within a sales and marketing team at KFC to help ensure that the family can maintain the lifestyle they have established without Eddie sacrificing his nights and weekends. It is an acceptable, comfortable style that provides few luxuries, but it does ensure priceless family time together. Unlike Eddie, however, Jennifer has the benefit of working for a "pride-builder" who emphasizes the nonmonetary benefits of engaging with interesting customers and respected colleagues. As a result, Jennifer takes real pride in working with her team to increase their "score" on the Colonel's dozen indicators of customer satisfaction.

Like many professional salespeople in almost every industry, Eddie works only as hard as necessary; he simply meets minimum expectations. He attends the weekly sales meetings where his supervisor provides information on specials and promotions and makes sure that Eddie understands what is required for him to remain within acceptable ranges on both quotas and product specials. Eddie, however, never goes the "extra mile" to earn more money, since that would seriously encroach on his thirty-five-hour-week lifestyle pattern. It is simply not a good trade-off from his point of view.

A few salespeople in Eddie's organization are, however, motivated by more than money. Invariably, their supervisors are instinctive pride-builders who become role models by building satisfying customer relationships, seizing on examples of satisfied customers to instill pride in others, and creating sales teams of colleagues who genuinely respect one another. As in Jennifer's situation, these supervisors seldom talk with their people about monetary incentives. As long as Eddie's supervisors concentrate entirely on money, they will not motivate him to higher levels of performance. Put him in a pride-building environment like Jennifer's, however, and he can be expected to behave more like his colleagues who take pride in their relationships and colleagues.

The company could, of course, increase Eddie's commission rates and bonus opportunities substantially to motivate him beyond his established level of performance—but it would require a level of compensation that is simply not economic for the food distribution business. As a result, they offer special incentives, such as annual trips for the top one hundred salesmen, as a less costly way of getting part of the sales force to seek higher levels of performance. It works for some, but not for others. Eddie occasionally wins a trip, but it is not a major factor in his motivation. Again, the trade-off is based on lifestyle patterns and acceptable (what will keep him from being laid off) performance results. Nor is the prospect of promotion particularly motivating, because it entails lots of added stress without the promise of much additional reward—and little prospect of feeling proud of what the job seems to require. Hence, both Eddie and the company have come to an implicit accommodation that neither motivates nor creates an expectation of higher-than-average performance. As long as the primary motivational mechanisms are monetary, this is unlikely to change.

Nor is Eddie particularly committed to the company or the job. Making the rounds of his accounts every day is a "drag" for him, and while he enjoys one or two of his customers, he views most of them as a pain in the neck. When he took the job, he respected his original supervisor, but those who came later were neither helpful nor admirable. Basically, they relied entirely on quota pressures and intimidating methods that created anxieties within their people, e.g., "If you don't make your quota, we'll find someone who will—no excuses here!" And every time Eddie's territory was modified (at least annually), he had to start anew to cultivate relationships with new customers. This pattern is common among companies whose sales efforts involve low-margin products. As a result, Eddie has changed jobs four times in the last ten years and periodically checks the job market to look for a better opportunity of more personal interest and less pressure. He is not particularly proud of his job, his coworkers, or his employer. So far, this perspective has been aggravated by role models who have focused only on monetary incentives; no one has made any serious effort to instill pride in Eddie by helping him to nourish lasting customer relationships or to work with respected colleagues. The amount of money he makes influences his decision to change jobs, but it does not motivate him to higher levels of performance within the job.

Fortunately for the family, Jennifer's job at KFC is very different. Although she originally took the job to earn extra money for the family, she is motivated to perform on the job primarily by nonmonetary factors—namely, the pride in her work and her fellow employees on which her leaders focus primary attention. Her current job is one of several that she has enjoyed at KFC over ten years; she is proud of what she does. The primary focus in her regional marketing team is on "making the RGM [Restaurant General Managers] Number One," the overriding KFC slogan and business priority. She takes great pride in helping RGMs assigned to her territory to penetrate their market and build their teams. Her "pride-builder" superiors have nourished her commitment to the company and what she believes she contributes to its performance. As a result, she has developed great respect for her managers, most of whom she considers real role models, and relishes what she does to make customers happy. In fact, she often willingly and cheerfully puts in extra hours on the weekends while Eddie is fishing with his buddies and has not even considered changing jobs for years now. Her motivation is unrelated to her compensation, since KFC knows how to create both pride and emotional commitment among its employees. Of course, it helps that Jennifer's pension benefits provide ample insurance for her family's retirement needs. Certainly, that realization helps keep her from looking elsewhere, but it is the intrinsic pride she feels in what she does and with whom she works that motivates her higher performance. Eddie cannot help but be a bit envious of Jennifer's good fortune.

For Eddie and Jennifer, materialistic pride is not the name of the game. They only care about earning enough to maintain a comfortable family lifestyle as they have defined it. Beyond that, Eddie has no choice but to look outside the job for his personal satisfactions (time with family and friends), whereas Jennifer finds many of her satisfactions in the workplace. In short, Eddie is no longer motivated by the earnings potential in his current job, cannot find a better one, and does not have the benefit of a "pride-builder" to help him develop pride in going beyond "minimum expectations." Jennifer is highly motivated by her job and her coworkers, has no interest in another job, and consistently performs above normal expectation levels. In Eddie's case, money is an ineffective motivator, and his supervisor is providing no other; in Jennifer's case, both an insightful supervisor and a "recognition and celebration" work environment instill pride rather than money as the primary motivator.

Many institutions have used high pay and materialistic pride with considerable success in building leadership positions in their industry, and the advantages are well known and accepted by most businessmen. Yet as Eddie and Jennifer's story has shown, they have obvious limits and drawbacks. The disadvantages are truly significant—particularly if you need the emotional commitment of key segments of your workforce to achieve your aspirations. And this is true whether you are the CEO of an enterprise of thousands of employees or a frontline supervisor who is concerned with motivating your unit of thirty salespeople. Emotional commitment of people to enterprise performance is invariably the result of institution-building or intrinsic pride—admittedly a much more difficult source of motivation in the short term, but in my experience a much more powerful source over time. Engaging the emotions of your people in ways that lead to superior unit or enterprise performance is well worth the effort.

CHAPTER 3

■

INSTILLING INSTITUTION-BUILDING PRIDE

Perhaps money and what it buys motivate you to excel at your job. But think for a moment about the exhilaration that you feel when a customer or client says that you saved the day for them by getting a critical product delivered when all others had failed. Or recall when one of your colleagues praised you strongly in front of your work group for winning over a difficult customer, thereby enabling them to meet their sales target; or when a respected superior singled you out as a role model of how others should deal with unexpected problems. Those feelings of pride are intrinsic to what you do, how you do it, and with whom you do it; they have little to do with money. More important, such feelings of pride are institution-building rather than self-serving. And, in most cases, they motivate people to excel far more effectively than money or position.

A few months ago, I shared a speakers' platform in Quantico, Virginia, with General John Ryan, USMC retired. He was speaking to a group of about ninety Wharton MBA candidates who had just experienced a remarkable day with the Marines in a specially designed "mock" run-through of the USMC Leadership Recognition and Combat Readiness Course. It was a shortened replica of what that course is really like; yet many of the Wharton students who participated in the day rated it as one of the better experiences of their two-year MBA program. The students were there to learn how the Marines think about and develop leadership capability, a skill for which the Corps has few peers. It would have been difficult to find a better speaker for these MBAs on the topic of leadership than General Ryan, a Medal of Honor winner in the Korean War.

Like most great leaders in any field, Ryan is a most unassuming individual. He genuinely believes others deserve more credit for courage under fire than he does. He introduced his remarks simply by first thanking his audience for their interest in Marine leadership approaches and then apologizing for what he thought might be an overly simplistic way for MBAs to think about leadership:

> I realize that as future business executives and potential leaders, you will have many challenging and complicating factors to worry about. In the Corps, however, we expect Marine leaders at all levels to worry *only* about two things. First and foremost is mission accomplishment: you must accomplish your mission—no matter what—unless the person who gave you that mission changes it. [Ryan's Medal of Honor was awarded for single-handedly destroying an enemy bridge after all other members of his platoon had been killed or incapacitated; he obviously understands mission accomplishment.]
>
> The second thing we want you to worry about is taking care of your troops—each and every one of them. We expect you to bring them home dead or alive under any and all conditions. That is why Marine platoons invariably have more survivors than other armed forces under similar battle conditions.
>
> As simple as these two requirements may sound, that is what Marine leadership is all about, and we should all be extremely proud of those who master it.

Intrinsic pride was apparent in every element of Ryan's remarks, just as pride is the fundamental motivational force for every aspect of the ways Marines are expected to behave. A Marine's pride, of course, is based upon a deep-seated belief in the values of honor, courage, and commitment. Corps values are what basic training for new recruits is all about. And it is the way the Corps expects all Marines to be rewarded—be they leaders, heroes, or frontline grunts. Those of us who seek to engage the emotional commitment of our employees have much to learn from the Marines.

DIFFERENT SOURCES OF INTRINSIC PRIDE

At Microsoft, the common source of pride is an intrinsic belief that "we make products that change the world." Industry competitors and software specialists often contest this claim, but it still persists throughout the company as a very real belief and source of pride. Employees remain convinced that they have led, are leading, and will continue to lead the world in making recognizably user-friendly software products that, as one technician proudly exclaimed, "all my friends and family can use."

Whatever you may think about Microsoft's market practices as highlighted in recent trial and press reports, the company has successfully motivated a large number of talented people from a variety of different disciplines for many years. To determine the sources of that motivation, we recently engaged several focus groups of employees from various parts of the company to respond to the following kinds of questions: What factors motivate you and others in the company to devote so much effort to your work? Why do people from different unique talent pools appear so willing to help one another in pursuit of very separate and different product projects? And why are people so mobile and receptive to transfer across different projects and programs?

The answers to our questions had little to do with annual earnings, bonuses, or even stock ownership value. Nor did the employees mention title, position, or material possessions of any kind. Rather, all comments reflected a burning pride in the products they were making, the projects they were part of, the talent they had access to, and the debatable proposition that "we are changing the world." The following comments excerpted from the focus groups we conducted reflect the different kinds of pride that motivate Microsoft people:

- *The products:* As one Microsoftie put it, "We work on products that everyone is likely to use—and I mean everyone. More than one hundred million people use Office, my product. People will stop me in the middle of a conversation and say, 'You worked on that [feature]?' It's instant respect and a great ego rush."

  "We are passionate about our products and really want them to succeed," continued another. "And succeeding is defined as being quickly adopted by our customers. One of the most frustrating things is having customers pay for a license for a product upgrade and then not using the upgrade. Even though we have made the sale, we have failed because the customer isn't using it."

  Another could hardly wait to tell his story: "I was at a product launch with customers. Three people at my table said to me, 'Thank you. You made my life so much easier.'

I can't tell you how good that made me feel—to have my work recognized and valued by a customer."

- *The project teams:* Project teams often came up as a source of pride. "People on my former project were so super-excited to be working on this application technology. They didn't really care where they were in the organization or what title they had—they just wanted to work with this technology. We still get together whenever a customer has a problem that needs to be solved."

- *The people:* "I really think that it's all about the talent. We have the best technical talent in the world, and what's even better is that anyone here can have access to all of it! I can send an e-mail to anyone in the company to get help as long as it's help for a good idea for a better product that the customer will want to buy. If I don't know who to go to, I can just e-mail billg [Bill Gates] and he will forward it to the right person. Amazing!"

- *The impossible dream:* One focus group member put it in a much more personal way: "I make products that even my grandmother uses! New software meant that I was able to send photos of my newborn son to my MSN community—including my grandmother—for them to see right away. This is really changing the world and I am a part of this. Even my grandmother . . .

  "It's not money. We must have over three thousand millionaires around here who are still burrowing away in their cubicles way into the night and through the weekend. If you think it's about money, think again. It is a matter of sheer pride in what we are creating."

That about summed it up.

A lot of people left Microsoft during the dark days of the federal government's attempt to convict the company of monopolistic practices. The company's stock plunged to a fraction of its former value while the verdict was in doubt. Yet a diligent journalistic search by an author at *Fortune* magazine who talked with dozens of former Microsoft employees during that period uncovered few who had a bad word to say about the company.[1] Moreover, a surprising number of ex-Microsofties still regarded their experiences there with great pride, e.g., "the best experience of my professional career." That experience, however, was all about what they learned, and what "change the world" products they worked on—not how much money they made.

As the preceding Microsoft comments illustrate, the sources of intrinsic (institution-building) pride are many, and some of them differ only subtly from those of materialistic pride. Nonetheless, the differences explain why intrinsic pride is such a powerful motivator. Let's examine a few of the more distinctive sources of institution-building pride within three basic categories that parallel Microsoft's specifics: pride in the results of your work, pride in how you work, and pride in whom you work with and for.

PRIDE IN THE RESULTS OF YOUR WORK

People can take pride in the results of any work that they do well. Also, a job well done is a source of both pride *and* dignity. Art Carney's classic comic television rendition of Norton, the sewer worker in *The Honeymooners* television show,

1. *Fortune,* July 10, 2000.

is a terrific example of a lovable character who actually took pride in doing a job that most of us would regard as both unpleasant and ignoble. In episode after episode, Norton would brag about both his buddies in the sewer and the special capabilities they had developed working in all the crap. Of course, Norton saw the sewer differently from most of us, but the television reruns are still making his countless fans laugh in creating normal workplace images out of the sewer. The following are elements of any job that can instill pride:

1. *The attributes of products you make:* If you are a designer of women's fashion clothing, the price of your products and the money you receive may be a clear indicator of the quality of your product. Perhaps you take pride in the money you get for your products and the material possessions you can obtain with that money. It is more likely, however, that Tom Ford (Gucci Group) or Giorgio Armani take greater pride in the distinctiveness of their designs and the approval of their discriminating buyers. The Davis Wire Company in California is an industry leader in a rather mundane field—wire and cable products. Yet an employee guiding a visitor through one of their plants will inevitably pause at the machine that produces chicken wire to explain with obvious pride the intricacies of the machine that makes it and the quality of that unremarkable commodity product. People really care about whatever kind of product they work on, and they take pride in doing it well. Manufacturing the best coiled-wire product is every bit as motivating to the workers at Davis Wire as designing Nicole Kidman's dress for the premiere of *Moulin Rouge* is to Tom Ford. The wise leader takes

advantage of that aspect of human nature in motivating his employees to higher levels of performance.

2. *The kind of work you do:* Not everyone can point to a specific product that is the result of her work. More and more people today work in professional service industries, and their specific work products are neither tangible nor visible. Knowledge workers typically fit this category. For them, intrinsic pride often stems from how they do their work and who pays attention to the knowledge they develop. At leading consulting firms such as the Boston Consulting Group, associates take great pride in the conceptual thinking, analytic rigor, and intellectual synthesis that lead to innovative recommendations that enable clients to succeed against tough competitors. They take great pride in the kind of work that leads to strategic breakthroughs.

Contributing to the invention of a "killer app" (an idea, approach, or application that renders competitive efforts obsolete) is a huge source of pride in many scientific or technology-based companies. Everybody wants to be a part of something that changes the game significantly—and often that is not a discrete product in the traditional sense. In fact, in most strategic consulting organizations, associates are reluctant to work on what they consider "process work" (i.e., organizational structure, systems design, or procedural simplification). They don't believe that kind of work is nearly as demanding intellectually or creatively as something more "strategic" or "technological." They are more easily motivated to tackle the challenging strategic problem (e.g., what new product market strategy for

Hewlett-Packard will best exploit their recent merger with Compaq?) than to work out the details of an effective human resource process (e.g., how can the merged company effect major change in frontline sales force behaviors?). Others, however, see the human aspects of so-called process work as more challenging than numeric analyses or strategic conceptualizations. Hence, they take great pride in how they are able to perceive and deal with the human elements of a business problem.

Alternatively, many craftsmen and tradespeople take great pride in what they do with their hands. They may produce rare products (e.g., great works of art) that have high monetary value, or they may simply be products that require careful attention to detail, such as weaving a rug or repairing an aircraft engine. Tim is a craftsman who works on restoration projects in Charleston, South Carolina. He has a rare ability to "fix anything," according to the people who employ him. It doesn't matter to Tim if the task involves hanging a new door, restoring an old stairway, or installing an expensive antique fireplace mantel. Whatever the task, he takes great pride in how it looks and works after he is finished. Needless to say, he is in constant demand within the Charleston historic district.

PRIDE IN *HOW* YOU WORK

The "how" refers to the set of values, standards, work ethics, and commitment you apply to your job. Even janitorial employees can take pride in how they mop the floor, wash the windows, or carry out other seemingly mundane aspects of their work. There is a right way to do almost any job, and the best workers take pride in mastering it.

Housekeepers at Marriott, for example, take great pride in how they make the beds and clean the rooms; they even have time standards that they are proud of achieving along with the reactions of customers as documented in Marriott's famous GSI (Guest Satisfaction Index). The GSI is a pervasive monthly compilation of how each employee is rated by the customers they come in contact with, either directly or indirectly. Maids, waiters, and bellboys as well as supervisors, managers, and executives know their GSI scores. The leader of the bell station group at the Marriott San Antonio resort hotel was well aware of how his group scored on the GSI from month to month. He also knew precisely where they stood relative to comparable hotels throughout the Marriott system, e.g.: "We were a close second to the Salt Lake City hotel last month, and we intend to beat their score and become number one within the next six months." He was proud of being number two among other bell stations in his category, but you can rest assured that the pride he feels in being in hot pursuit of number one goes well beyond the pride of being number two.

It is somewhat surprising to find the product that people take pride in delivering may not be of high value. Nonetheless, they can take pride in "doing it right." For example, Colonel Sanders had a list of twelve elements of service, known as the Colonel's Dozen, which became virtually inviolate throughout his outlets long before he sold the brand to "big business" interests. Even after several different corporate owners, which have included R.J. Reynolds, PepsiCo, and Tricon, the Colonel's Dozen remains alive and well, despite the demise of the Colonel himself. This simple checklist is the basis for what KFC considers the right way to run a family-affordable chicken-dinner business, and the better franchisees still take pride in maintaining a crew that adheres to the Colonel's way. In fact, the company now has built into its managerial process an inspection check based upon these dozen tasks.

The list is almost as famous internally with KFC employees as the infamous secret formula for fried chicken is with customers. As a result, the entire KFC organization takes pride in applying and protecting the twelve elements. Again, money does not enter this formula for success at KFC; the people feel at least as much pride about receiving the president's "rubber chicken" award as they do about receiving their annual bonus. The award was established by David Novak when he was CEO to recognize individuals who demonstrate unusual commitment to the KFC values, provide consistent support to restaurant general managers, and deliver unique value to customers. While the rubber chicken is awarded somewhat at the president's whim, it is very meaningful to the recipients. The chicken award probably costs no more than $10; yet people who win one display it proudly at their workstation or desk for years.

If how you work is an important source of pride and motivation for you, it is likely that you pay close attention to one or more of the following three elements: applying self-discipline, aligning personal values with institutional values, and creating a strong work ethic.

1. *Applying self-discipline:* The self-disciplined employee needs little help from others to find and pursue sources of intrinsic pride. Lance Armstrong, Tour de France

winner and cancer survivor, probably doesn't need much more than his own determination to motivate his incredible training regimen. True entrepreneurs are so determined to build their own business that they often forget about the derivative benefit of creating a successful company: making lots of money. Great artists (be they painters, actors, or authors) learn to discipline themselves to meet their own impossible standards of excellence.

We found self-discipline (usually enabled by the wise application of top-down and peer-enforcing discipline) in every "peak performance" situation that we researched. The Marines, of course, exemplify the motivational power of self-discipline. Somewhat more surprisingly, however, completely unmilitary institutions such as Southwest Airlines and KFC also know that the full power of self-discipline depends upon its integration with both top-down and peer-enforced discipline. It all starts at the top, and by the time employees at SWA and KFC are fully on board, they recognize the importance of self-discipline in the work environment they are joining.

2. *Aligning personal and institutional values:* Most people, unfortunately, have not developed an instinctive ability to identify and pursue energizing sources of pride on their own. And the organizations they work for don't have a work culture that is as emotionally motivating as at Southwest Airlines or Marriott. In addition, a great many jobs are inherently boring and do not naturally inspire energy or pride. Hence, these people need a bit more help along this path than either the naturally

self-motivated individuals or the employees of emotionally motivating institutions.

Unfortunately, a great many supervisors go the other way by resorting to intimidation, pressure, and other anxiety-producing tactics. For example, a recent article in the *New York Times* reported that several Wal-Mart employees were ordered to punch out after an eight-hour shift and then continue working for no pay. The *Times* also reported that Wal-Mart store managers in six states have locked the doors at closing time, according to some employees, forcing all present to remain for an hour or more of unpaid labor. A company spokesman says it is Wal-Mart's policy "to pay its employees properly for the hours they work." Yet the article cites several examples of after-hour mandatory sessions that are the target of employee lawsuits. While these accusations have yet to be proved in court, they are illustrative of practices by managers who rely on pressure rather than pride to get extra effort from their people.[2]

My daughter-in-law, Keena, worked for a sales supervisor who purposely created anxiety on every visit to her office by pushing a by-the-numbers system that did not reflect significant territory differences. In fact, the prospect of Karen's visits caused Keena many sleepless nights just worrying about the pressure tactics she knew would be applied. Unfortunately, Karen reflected a leadership system based upon pushing to boost near-term numbers no matter what. As a result, despite being one

2. Barbara Ehrenreich, "Another Day, Another Indignity," *New York Times*, June 30, 2002, op-ed, p. 15.

of the top producers in the company, Keena left the job within a year to find a less anxiety-producing job.

While it is true that in their early days new Marine recruits face anxiety-producing techniques, it isn't long before pride takes over. Marine leaders know that the Corps values of character, courage, and commitment that instill intrinsic pride are much more motivating than pressure tactics based on intimidation and fear. That is why the Marines devote their entire recruit boot camp to inculcating their core values rather than standard military training and skill building. Unless new recruits can align their personal values with the USMC values, they cannot become Marines. The same holds true at Southwest Airlines, although their training and indoctrination programs differ markedly from those of the Marines. But the fundamental objective of aligning institutional and personal values is the same because those sources of pride ensure high performance in both institutions.

3. *Creating a strong work ethic within your work group:* Regardless of the value system, there is no substitute for plain old hard work. Yet the world is full of bright people who assume that a superior intellect is all they need to make their mark in the world. I have encountered many of them in my profession. Only those who apply themselves with rigor and actually learn "how to get things done" will make significant, worthwhile contributions to the institutions that hire them. Unfortunately, the "work ethic" of many workforce entrants is not particularly admirable. Far too many are looking for an easy way to get by, and a great many employers

accept that attitude as inevitable. Some very bright people, surprisingly, take great pride in figuring out how to beat the system, rather than applying their talents to increase their own performance and that of their colleagues and employers. As a result, the entitlement mind-set can spread like ivy unless and until leaders take steps to prevent it.

How you do your work clearly matters. Not only does it influence the effectiveness and efficiency of what you produce, but it also becomes a source of pride that can motivate you to higher levels of performance. It can be as important as the pride you take in the results of your work, as well as the pride instilled in you by those you work with and for.

PRIDE IN *WHOM* YOU WORK WITH AND FOR

Most of us derive considerable job satisfaction from the people we work with—be they superiors, subordinates, or peers. At companies like Avon, Goldman Sachs, Marriott, and KFC, determining personal values and characteristics is a critical factor in recruitment and selection; intellect is only one small criterion. These companies create terms that highlight their "kind of person," such as "Avon Ladies," which become labels of great respect both inside and outside the enterprise. They are seeking what Daniel Goleman terms emotional intelligence rather than sheer intellect.[3] People who work at companies like those are proud of being the kind of person that the enterprise pursues.

3. Daniel Goleman, *Emotional Intelligence: Why It Can Matter More than IQ* (New York: Bantam Books, 1995).

For example, at 3M, many workers take great pride in working in teams. Despite its recent financial difficulties, the company is still famous for its dedication to innovation over several decades, and many of their inventions are the result of real-team efforts. In our research for *Peak Performance* we encountered a good example of how 3M teams thrive on pride to create new products and services for customers.

John Owens was a research specialist and team leader in the fluorochemicals division at 3M. John first worked at 3M as an intern while in college and joined the company full-time after graduating in 1984. He says that growing up in the Twin Cities, he "always wanted to work for 3M," because of its good reputation in the community. He had many neighbors who worked for the company, and they spoke proudly of 3M as a place where researchers were "allowed to pursue their scientific interests" without too much interference or "micromanagement." Virtually everyone John knew at 3M was proud to work for the company.

In his position at the time of our research, John played the role of both scientist and manager. With the one-third of his time that he spent as a team leader, John oversaw a nine-person, cross-functional group responsible for commercializing new product applications of HFE chemicals (CFC replacements). Commercialization teams act as a kind of "bridge" between new chemical development (concepts) and business application teams, which support existing products once they have been commercialized. John's view of how pride produces team performance is fairly compelling. The team decides by consensus to set "stretch" goals and to work hard to meet them. While management has some say in determining timelines and goals for the project, the team members are primarily responsible for developing their own work plan. Far from "padding" the project to add in extra time, the team pushes itself to work harder. They are motivated by two important sources of pride, according to John:

- "People take pride in being able to follow through on their work . . . the team members want to do as good of a job as they can and work to the best of their abilities."

- "Any employee who takes pride in his work will want to complete assignments so as not to let the team down. . . . We don't have much trouble with low performers, because nobody wants to look bad in front of their coworkers."

Performing teams invariably reflect this kind of pride, but it is also evident in larger organizational constructs. Enterprises that capitalize on this pride in motivating their people usually pay close attention to the following three factors:

1. *The kind of people the enterprise seeks to attract:* Pride in the type of people that your employer attracts and retains works both ways. You strive hard to live up to those attributes and expectations. And because the organization recognizes that you and others are proud of working with them, they try hard to set the right example as well as to create the right expectations. When both sides—employees and employers—exhibit behavior that leads to higher enterprise performance, everybody benefits. Not too many years ago, Southwest Airlines could claim close to 150,000 applications for 5,000 job openings annually. They took full advantage of that situation by developing a methodology that

would ensure a certain kind of employee. Interestingly, they were much less interested in where you went to school or what your grades were than they were in your character, personality, sense of humor, and dedication to excel within the low-cost service system that constitutes SWA's competitive advantage.

For example, SWA screening includes a series of interviews and dialogues that are designed to bring out the applicant's personality and enthusiasm for working with a difficult diversity of customers, as well as his sense of humor and general energy level. They also look for the atypical fun answer: one recruit described her best attribute for the job as "bounciness"; another swore that his primary reason for wanting the job was that his sister taunted him with "You're wasting your time applying to SWA, because you're no fun." In job interviews with other companies, these kinds of answers would either be ignored or classify the respondent as "too frivolous"; at SWA, they get you the job. The employees of Southwest Airlines are proud of working with people whose relative "quotient for silliness" makes them fun for customers and colleagues alike.

McKinsey & Company, Inc. sustains one of the premier pools of business talent; hundreds of associates and partners alike take great pride in the caliber of talent with whom they work. The partners, of course, are also particularly proud of the prestigious list of companies McKinsey serves. More often than not, however, McKinsey associates place more emphasis on the quality of talent whom they perceive makes up the bulk of the professional staff. They thrive on working with people whose intelligence and character they respect and from whom they believe they can really learn and grow personally as well as professionally. Like Microsoft employees, ex-McKinsey people will invariably mention the quality of the people in describing what they were most proud of during their time with the firm and how motivated they were to earn the respect of such talented colleagues.

2. *The caliber of people in specific work groups:* While this tends to be a function of the kind of people a company hires, the characteristics of specific work groups are often unique. If you have ever been a member of a real team, you know that its members were extremely proud of one another's capabilities, as well as of what they were able to accomplish as a group. Real teams can be found in almost any organization, regardless of its leadership philosophy or workplace culture. Even companies with strong monetary reward cultures such as investment banks and venture capital firms cannot snuff out all real-team efforts, although such efforts are certainly less prevalent in those environments. Nonetheless, it is possible for small groups in such enterprises to be motivated by their intrinsic pride in being part of a small group of people they truly respect and admire.

The Sony Dream Team described in *Business Week* in January 1990 provides an interesting illustration.[4] In the early 1990s, top management was dabbling with the notion of introducing a personal computer for the business office market, although at that time it was not a top priority. In the spirit of "let the skunk works prevail," Sony dispatched a group of "misfit" engineers to

4. *Business Week,* January 15, 1990, 76.

explore that opportunity. (Sony apparently had nothing better to do with them at the time.) Since management seemed to be paying no attention to them, these self-labeled misfits decided to create a new engineering workstation rather than the office computer they were supposed to be inventing. After all, they were engineers who could get a lot more excited about a product that they would actually use in their own professional pursuits. Despite the clear realization that they could expect little in the way of monetary reward or recognition for building the wrong product, they pursued it with incredible zeal. The result: a superior engineering workstation that was ready for market in less than two years and that within five years had captured over 20 percent of the Japanese market for engineering computers. It was one of the most successful new product introductions in Japan's computer history. The entire motivation for the self-named Dream Team was pride in their unique product challenge and pride in their colleagues for taking the risk.

Team motivation is surprisingly devoid of personal chemistry. You don't have to like your colleagues socially to respect their work capabilities and be proud of working with them on a team—particularly when you believe strongly in the end product you are pursuing, as did the Dream Team. Companies that sustain multiple real teams in critical parts of their business invariably benefit from the motivation members of these teams derive from simply being proud of working with their teammates. I have never researched nor worked with an enterprise that did not have at least a few real teams somewhere in their organization. Of course, those organizations that recognize and encourage the members of such teams get a lot more real teams than those who ignore them.

3. *The legacy and history of the enterprise:* Never underestimate the motivational value of a rich institutional history. The rich local history of the Oldsmobile V-8 engine line at the General Motors Lansing plant motivated the workers right through to the end when they vowed to make their last V-8 engine the best V-8 engine ever. Closing that line meant the loss of many jobs, but that didn't stop the plant employees' pride from motivating them to exceed expectations. Even companies with a relatively short duration of industry leadership, such as Southwest Airlines (fifteen to twenty years), The Home Depot (twenty to twenty-five years), or Microsoft (ten to fifteen years), have developed large segments of their workforces that are not only aware of the history, but also extremely proud of it—and strongly motivated to perpetuate the legacy.

Great institutions consciously work to encourage feelings of intrinsic pride in both personal and enterprise performance throughout their workforce. When Bernie Marcus told his employees that "you are president of your aisle" at The Home Depot, he really meant it; and they believed him.[5] In Bernie's mind, being president of your aisle means that you think and act as if you own the products on those shelves and that the customers who wander down the aisle are literally yours to delight or disappoint. You want to be proud of what

5. Bernie Marcus was succeeded by Arthur Blank as CEO in 1997 during the time of our research. Robert Nardelle became CEO in 2000.

you sell, proud of the customers you are able to attract, and proud of their satisfaction with what you do for them. If the products on your aisle aren't as good or appealing to customers as those in a comparable aisle of a competitor across the road, it is up to you to do something about it by finding ways to get different products, different service levels, or different customers. You don't get to blame the system, the economy, or the weather.

WHY INSTITUTION-BUILDING PRIDE IS OVERLOOKED

Why institution-building pride is so often overlooked as a motivational force is a bit perplexing. Certainly, the natural appeal of self-serving pride and the relative ease of relying on monetary incentives are contributing reasons. As a result, most organizations do not pay nearly as much attention to institution-building pride as a primary source of energy or motivation as they do to self-serving pride. For example, few "value statements" even mention the word *pride.* Leadership templates and development programs largely ignore the need to help potential leaders develop "pride-building" skills, tools, and techniques. Pride is simply "assumed" to be the result of an achievement rather than a force that can be actively cultivated or nourished to motivate increasingly higher achievement. Finally, and most unfortunately, extreme and conspicuous examples of self-serving pride can mislead people into associating institution-building pride with arrogant attitudes and behaviors.

As a result, many companies inadvertently plow under the seeds of institution-building pride within their workforces. Insecurity and intimidation are alive and well as managers focus on replacing mediocre workers rather than finding nonmonetary ways to motivate them. The spirit of "Chainsaw Al" Dunlap lives on; it's a lot easier to replace people than to build up natural sources of institution-building pride that will motivate them to higher levels of personal and enterprise performance. Macho leaders of both genders trumpet the common intimidating threat "The reward for improving your performance is keeping your job!" Yet recurring layoffs and head-count reductions are seldom events in which workers take pride. Negative feedback dominates evaluation programs, and few managers know how to give feedback that motivates rather than threatens. As a result, one of America's premier executive coaches, Marshall Goldsmith, recently came up with the appealing notion of "feed forward." Goldsmith's notion of feed forward is simply to focus evaluation discussions on the good things that can result from a different set of behaviors going forward (and thereby to trigger the anticipation of pride) rather than to belabor the bad things that are the result of current behaviors. Simple as it sounds, this notion seldom prevails in most companies.

Yet in virtually every organizational unit, large or small, you can find the natural intrinsic "pride-builders" who work relentlessly on engaging the emotional commitment and pride of the people who work with them. While such leaders are in short supply at every level of the company, they do exist. However, it takes much more than lip service to increase the supply and capitalize on its performance potential. You start by encouraging leaders at all levels to pay close attention to, and diligently cultivate, what employees already take pride in. It is important to make heroes and role models out of such people. It is even more important to find ways to transfer their skills and techniques and tools to others. Consider the case of Charlotte Fludd, a rare, self-motivated employee whose remarkable level of performance seemed to defy replication.

EVERY COMPANY HAS A CHARLOTTE!

In almost every organization you can find the "hidden Charlottes." They are employees of modest stature whose performance and personal contributions to enterprise success far exceed reasonable expectation based on their compensation or hierarchical position. Invariably these people are motivated by intrinsic pride in what they do and how they do it; they are remarkable institution builders. As one pride-builder at General Motors said, "They bring it with them; the trick is not to cause them to lose it when they enter the workplace."

When we first discovered Charlotte Fludd, she was a second-level supervisor in the collections department call center of a credit card business owned by a large U.S. bank. She supervised fifty people trying to collect from customers who were seriously delinquent on their accounts. Four other groups of people in Charlotte's section of the bank did exactly the same job, but Charlotte's group outperformed their counterparts by over $1 million a month in profit contribution. Clearly, there was something to be learned from Charlotte, but it turned out to be easier said than done. For one thing, Charlotte herself could not articulate how she did it. What was painfully clear, however, was how much pride Charlotte took in what her group did. Unfortunately, neither she nor her superiors could figure out how to teach those elements of Charlotte's approach that would work for others.

So she remained the classic one-of-a-kind enigma that every enterprise has that causes leaders to conclude, "it's magic."

Actually, magic is a good analogy for pride-building capability. When you see the magician in action, you can't figure out how he does the trick. If you go behind stage, however, and watch his actions carefully, perhaps with some insightful help from others who know the magic, it is not so mysterious. Even the most mysterious magic tricks can be broken down into their essential elements, and with hard work and practice, others can and do learn how to do it. So it is with pride: the seemingly mysterious instinct that pride-builders have is actually a teachable skill that others can master just like managing by the numbers.

Not surprisingly, senior management had come to view Charlotte as a lucky accident, someone with magical powers who could never be replicated. They had made several attempts to have Charlotte convey her secrets to others, but these efforts focused primarily on best-practice comparisons that left her colleagues perplexed and caused them to feel of secondary importance.

Luckily, a determined executive decided to go backstage and study the act seriously. He commissioned a rigorous economic and anthropological analysis of Charlotte's behavior. The analysis revealed three or four things that Charlotte did that others did not do—and a similar number of things that she did not do that others did. For example, Charlotte maintained a rather strange "calendar" consisting of dozens of sheets of paper and notes assembled in no apparent order or framework. Close observation revealed that her "calendar" was a relatively simple way for her to apply a systematic scientific approach of changing one variable at a time (e.g., frequency of call or sequence of messages) while holding all other variables constant. Thus, she could determine for different categories of customer what had the highest probability of working. Charlotte had no scientific or statistical training, but she was applying both disciplines to her performance challenge. No wonder it looked like magic to her managers and colleagues. Once that kind of factual base was established, however, it became relatively easy to create a set of variable testing techniques that others could benefit from and take pride in applying and mastering. The result was over $50 million annually to the bank's bottom line.

In this case, simply exposing others to Charlotte's intrinsic pride was not enough to create a significant performance result. However, once the basis of her performance was determined in behavioral terms, management could put in place the mechanisms that would allow others to change their behaviors and take pride in mastering new skills as well as in the resulting improvement in profits for the bank. All of this happened without significant monetary incentive. Simply put, people take pride in mastering new capabilities that motivate them to achieve higher levels of performance than they ever thought possible. You cannot expect the prospect of more money to motivate them in the same way, because the money won't help them learn new skills. But the knowledge that those new skills will lead to better performance and pride in the prospect of that performance is incentive enough.

CHAPTER 4

■

HOW MOTIVATIONS DIFFER AT THE FRONT LINE

■

Edward Snell is an upper-level professional in the global foreign-exchange group of a large financial services institution. He is a type A personality; e.g., he can be found at his desk from seven-twenty in the morning until eight or nine in the evening almost every day he is not out of town on business. His job requires him to travel a lot, and his wife considers it a rare event if he is not working at home on the weekend. His cell phone is turned on constantly, FedEx packages arrive every Saturday morning, and he often rushes to get his bag packed for the Sunday-afternoon flight to London or Hong Kong.

Ed's motivation is hardly in question. If you ask him why he works at such a frantic pace, he will tell you that it's the nature of his profession and the only way he will get ahead in the company. And for Ed, getting ahead is what it is all about; climbing the corporate hierarchy to higher-and-higher-paying opportunities is how he thinks about success. He understands exactly what he contributes to the bank's foreign exchange earnings and how important that contribution is to its return on invested capital.

He wants to be a top executive before he is forty-five, and he hopes one day to run a global line of business for one of the leading financial institutions—either his current employer or a comparable one. While he likes the company, he frequently considers other job opportunities and tells his friends that if he is not promoted within the next year or two, he will undoubtedly relocate. In fact, this is the third major financial institution that he has worked for in the last six years; each move was motivated by the chance to advance more rapidly in both compensation and position. Nonetheless, Ed is proud of his position in the global exchange group, and he savors that he is one of the highest-paid professionals in the group. He is very conscious of his annual bonus as well as his overall compensation increases relative to others in the group. He considers anything less than a 20 percent annual increase completely unacceptable. He knows what "the pros" in his field earn, and he regards himself as one of the better producers, so he expects to be paid accordingly.

Ed's pride in what he earns also reflects itself in his lifestyle. His family lives in one of the most desirable areas of Greenwich, Connecticut, and his children attend one of the better private schools. His wife has a Cadillac sport utility vehicle for doing the family errands, and Ed drives a BMW sports model to and from the train station. The Snells entertain regularly and are proud of the kinds of people that come to their parties—mostly well-heeled executives and customers of the bank, along with respected community leaders of Greenwich. There is little question that Ed is a valuable, highly motivated investment professional of the bank that employs him. There is also little question that money and position are at the heart of his motivation.

A few floors down in Ed's building is an executive assistant named Burton Jenkins, who works for Martin Zallone, one of Ed's executive colleagues in the trust department of the bank. Burton is a much-respected employee who could probably work for any executive in the department. He likes, respects, and enjoys working for Martin. No task is too difficult or menial for Burt to tackle with a smile. He is often sought out by people for whom he doesn't officially work to help with unexpected challenges such as setting up emergency client meetings, arranging for special leadership lunches, helping a professional analyst fix malfunctions in her PC software, or delivering critical messages and reports to clients. Burton is proud of the diversity of tasks he is called upon to do, as well as the range of people who seek him out. Like Ed, Burt seldom limits his work to an eight-hour day, puts in lots of unpaid overtime in the evenings, and is always there when needed.

Burt lives in an apartment with two other roommates in lower Manhattan and takes the subway to and from work. He is an aspiring actor and participates in a local theatrical group when he is not working—but he seldom allows his acting life to interfere with his job. Burt has little if any interest in being promoted, since he likes working for Martin and his colleagues. Nor is he particularly concerned about his title or compensation as long as the normal annual increases keep him ahead of inflation. While he'd like to earn more money to stay a bit further above the basic subsistence level in New York City, money is not his primary motivation. With only a junior college education, he realizes that making "big money" is not a realistic aspiration.

Nonetheless, he is proud of being a working New Yorker who makes do on whatever he earns and still knows how to enjoy the great city. He was deeply disturbed by the World Trade Center attacks on September 11, 2001, and worked at various volunteer needs in his neighborhood. If you ask him why he puts so much time in on the job, he would probably tell you that he enjoys being there, likes and respects the people he works with, and believes what he does is important to a lot of people. Everybody in his work group has the highest respect for Burt's reliability, initiative, and attitude—and he is proud of how he is valued by superiors, peers, and subordinates (three junior clerical assistants). Burt has worked for the bank for nearly eight years and has no intention of leaving. While he certainly worries about the lay-offs that come thundering across the bank every so often, he is probably one of the last employees who needs to worry.

Most large organizations have lots of people like Edward Snell and Burton Jenkins. The Edward Snells can typically be found within the upper levels—both physically and hierarchically—whereas the Burton Jenkinses are more prevalent within the lower levels and throughout the broad base of employees. Obviously, there are exceptions to this pattern in both directions. But what motivates upper-level executives and professional leaders is considerably different from what motivates frontline employees and supervisors. This difference is even more pronounced when a company is not doing particularly well. The remaining sections of this chapter explore some of the most important differences between motivation at the top and down the line. A capsule picture of the Aetna medical insurance business serves to illustrate some of these differences rather dramatically, particularly because of the way they came into focus during difficult times.

THE AETNA STORY: RESTORING THE PRIDE

The Aetna story begins with values. It is easy to understand how institutional values generate pride in companies that can trace their current success to years of adherence to those values. But values can also provide a powerful source of pride in companies such as Aetna that must struggle through difficult turnaround situations. Moreover, a credible if not compelling set of values are most important at the front line where the workforce needs a positive counterbalance to troublesome near-term results.

Aetna is one of the oldest and largest health insurance companies in the world. Despite nearly 150 years of leading its industry in providing reliable insurance for individual and group life, property, and casualty, as well as health care, the company has suffered through a series of difficulties over the last ten years. Their historic advertising slogan and motto "Aetna, I'm glad I met ya!" is no longer the household indicator of quality service that it once was. The most recent trauma for the company occurred after an extensive period of unsatisfying diversification acquisitions led to a spin-off of the health care business that retains the brand name. Nonetheless, Aetna's earnings and market position suffered badly, many people lost their jobs, and a new CEO and senior leadership team had to be installed.

Throughout the transition, Aetna's fundamental values of integrity and service have remained an essential part of the company's culture even as those values were being tarnished. Moreover, pride in the company's basic values has served as a core motivational element that the new leadership team uses in helping people deal with the public outrage at the treatment patients have received at the hands of many health maintenance organizations (HMOs). Far too many HMOs sacrificed customer service, patient care, and even common courtesy in favor of controlling and reducing medical costs. Aetna still faces an awesome two-pronged task: (1) to turn around its operational effectiveness in both cost and customer-service terms, and (2) to shape and execute a new strategy that will enable it to regain and sustain its historic leadership legacy. The new CEO, Jack Rowe, is a former medical doctor and geriatrics specialist. He probably knows better than most that unless the company can rekindle the pride latent in its employee base and spread that pride to its customers, sponsors, and providers, the turnaround cannot succeed. It is no wonder, therefore, that in addition to restoring financial performance, his initial efforts have heavily focused on "resurrecting" a modern version of the old Aetna values (see following chart).

At a recent gathering of hundreds of Aetna employees, Rowe explained the mission, strategy, and values of what he refers to as "the new Aetna." The story was somewhat involved, so it was hardly surprising when one of the members of the audience, a loyal and valued employee named Liz Young, raised an obvious question: "Dr. Rowe, can you help me understand what this all means?"

Rowe pondered the question he knew was probably in everyone's mind, then said, "Well, Liz, it is all about restoring the pride." The comment prompted standing applause from the entire audience because that's what they instinctively knew they needed. A few days later when Rowe announced that Ron Williams would become the president, reflecting his stellar performance in the early stages of the turnaround, it is significant that Williams clearly stated his promise to "restore the pride." And according to Dr. Rowe, the senior leadership team now introduces every appearance before employees with the same compelling phrase.

150 Years of Value-Based Pride at Aetna

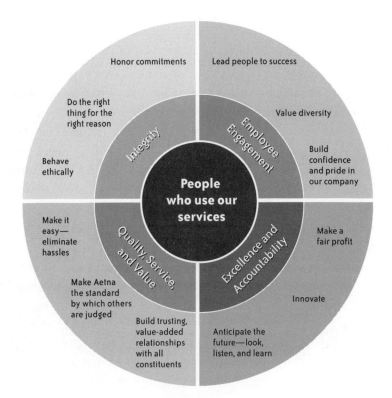

BACKGROUND

Aetna was founded in the Morgan Coffee House in Hartford, Connecticut, as a fire insurer, amending its charter the following year to include life insurance. It became the Aetna Life Insurance Company in 1853, and the brand has been an icon for exemplary insurance practices for much of the time since then. Despite the economic turmoil that has plagued Aetna in recent years, its legacy of customer care, quality service, and physician capability remains a source of latent pride for many of today's employees.

Few enterprises have lasted as long as Aetna. The U.S. Marine Corps, born in 1775, and Du Pont, which marked its bicentennial in 2002, probably head the list. Colgate-Palmolive (1806), Procter and Gamble (1837), and The New York Times Company (1851) also come to mind as institutions with histories that exceed 150 years. But even such venerable household names as Ford and General Mills fall well short of that mark. Obviously, being part of a rich history instills pride in employees, but the pride that motivates performance is a bit different at the front line from what it is within upper-level management ranks. It is important to consider both the good times and the bad times at Aetna as context for the motivation and pride challenges the company faces today.

The company was actually named after Mount Etna, a volcano in Sicily, in which its founders saw analogies of strength and durability. Had they been more clairvoyant, they might also have seen analogies to the volcanic eruptions—since Aetna has certainly been through more than a few. Thomas Enders became Aetna's first full-time employee in 1854 and its second president in 1872. He was a major advocate of expanding geographic coverage to include the "New West" frontier. He fought a difficult battle to initiate a system of mutual ownership to stem sales losses and to ensure business viability and lobbied his board to establish the first insurance policy that paid dividends to policyholders. These critical shifts in strategy enabled Aetna to become one of the nation's leading life insurers by the turn of the century.

Aetna's roots are inextricably intertwined with major events in U.S. history. It bonded the construction of the Hoover Dam as well as the construction of the National Archives Building in Washington, D.C. It has insured countless legendary characters, including Jimmy Stewart and Henry Fonda of Hollywood screen fame, as well as America's original seven astronauts, whose 1963 historic twenty-two-orbit flight capped the pioneering Mercury program.

When serious disasters struck, Aetna was there to help. On April 18, 1906, "the Great Earthquake of 1906" hit San Francisco, resulting in a fire that burned down over 15 percent of the city in three days. The losses included five hundred deaths, scores of buildings destroyed, and property losses of over $350 million. Senator and Aetna president Bulkeley declared on the floor of the U.S. Senate that the company had paid millions of dollars to cover its share of damages and claims from the fires. A claims representative from another company wrote to his home office praising Aetna's responsiveness, outstanding service, and industry standard of excellence in the face of significant losses.

Aetna history buffs tell the story of Richard Wheeler, a traveling salesman and inventor of Wheeler's IML Compound for healing wounds. Wheeler's troubles began in

February 1906 aboard a steamer between Los Angeles and San Francisco, where he fell during rough seas and sustained head injuries that disabled him for several months. Shortly thereafter, a favorite grandchild died; and as if that were not enough, the San Francisco quake destroyed his home and all of his earthly possessions. Thanks to the committed field agents and home office employees at Aetna, Richard and his family received relief within weeks of the fire and were able to rebuild a life otherwise on the rocks. This kind of story is a lot more meaningful to frontline people than President Bulkeley's speech about corporate monetary losses before the U.S. Senate. And stories of past value-based deeds by Aetna agents still stir feelings of pride within Aetna and were featured at a recent Aetna leadership conference in June of 2001.

For a proud institution like Aetna, the last decade has been painful. As part of the ill-fated surge into HMOs, the company has been one of the primary targets of relentless attacks by investors, the business press, and the public alike. These public criticisms have been painful to endure at all levels of the organization. Not only did financial performance decline dramatically when the HMO approach withered, but the public press took dead aim against what was perceived as an excessive industry focus on cutting medical costs at the expense of patient service and physician relationships. Aetna has been at the center of this attack, despite its recent determined efforts to restore customer confidence, rebuild patient trust, and strengthen physician loyalty. During the 1990s, the company went through at least four major changes at top management levels as its board pushed hard for better performance. The medical insurance businesses were spun off as the more attractive financial services business was acquired by ING.

Not surprisingly, during the late 1990s the primary motivational emphasis within Aetna's medical insurance businesses has been on getting back to an acceptable, if not yet attractive, return to the shareholders and investors. Management by the numbers within a command-and-control approach was the primary motivational tool at the top; and top executives were understandably focused on medical costs, revenue quality, and return on capital. While these metrics were clear to the front line, they were hardly a primary source of pride and emotional commitment to longer-term aspirations for the "New Aetna" that CEO John Rowe envisions. Under his leadership, the company is clearly resurrecting the Aetna values of old and launching a major effort to restore pride and build emotional commitment among all employees. Aetna's experience shows why pride is actually more important as a motivational force during trying times and difficult challenges than it is during periods of attractive growth and profitability. It also illustrates how important value-based pride is to employees during difficult times. The following two short stories highlight how savvy Aetna managers instilled institution-building pride among their people when corporate results were discouraging, as well as how different sources of pride were used to motivate the front line.

A PERSONAL FRONTLINE CONNECTION

Rich Schlichting is a claims manager for Aetna in Middletown, Connecticut, who knows how to motivate frontline people. While his basic philosophy of paying attention to each and every person can certainly apply at upper-management levels, it is really critical at the front line.

"Leveraging my time" is not nearly as important in Rich's leadership approach as it is for most executives.

Rich is a soft-spoken man whose sincerity is obvious from the start. As with most unassuming leaders, his style belies how much his people admire and respect him. Nor does it indicate the consistently high levels of performance that his unit has delivered in the three years he has managed it—three of the hardest years in Aetna's 150-year history. Somehow he seems too soft-spoken for all that. At the heart of Rich's ability to motivate is his sincere passion for his people. He believes in and cares about all his people, and how they feel about their jobs. As a result, his leadership compass is always focused on what he can do to make them proud of what they are doing. Like most pride-builders, it all seems pretty simple and straightforward to him: "You just need to treat your employees like people." As simple as that seems, Rich is the first to point out that keeping people motivated during troubling times can be a full-time, demanding task.

When Rich speaks of treating his employees like people, he has several things in mind, starting with being easily approachable, something he worked to establish from the start. For example, his people remember clearly when he first came to the unit. He sought out their expertise, acknowledged their experience in areas where he was weak, and met with each of them to learn what they could teach him about the business. In short, he tried to make it clear to each person that "you really matter here."

This early emphasis on connecting with and learning from his people has repaid itself many times over. His employees not only respect his sincere interest in their inputs, but they want to work with him as a collaborator. They know that he values their ideas and their knowledge, and they are vocally proud of his confidence in them. When they have questions, they are comfortable and confident going to him as a mentor and a teacher. Being serious about listening to people has clearly conveyed his respect for each employee and planted the seeds of personal pride in each of them, i.e., "my opinion really counts."

Rich is always aware of how his people feel about their work, what frustrates or hinders them, and when they need personal attention and coaching to get through a tough task. As one noted: "Rich will never ask you to do anything that he wouldn't do himself, and he'll fight to get you what you need to succeed. . . . I know that he's committed to me, [so] I want . . . to do the best work possible for him."

Rich works to reinforce a sense of ownership and pride in his employees by (1) communicating constantly to be sure his people understand the broader "why" behind their work, (2) tying their day-to-day activities to the larger goals of the unit and the company, and (3) showing them how their everyday efforts are progressing toward these larger goals. Most important, perhaps, when times were really tough for Aetna as a whole, employees appreciated Rich's refusal to sugarcoat the truth, while at the same time putting the reality of that hardship in the larger context of turning the company around through hard work and daily progress. His integrity about the problems gave them confidence in his convictions about the future.

On both an individual and group level, Rich aggressively seeks out ways to recognize people. Since his group is involved directly with customers, few sources of pride are as credible as customer accolades. So whenever someone's good work receives praise or thanks from a customer, Rich publicizes it among all of his employees. Thus, he gets employees to take pride and ownership in their work along the way as well as when major "pride-inducing" milestones occur.

Rich is also a strong and active advocate for his employees with respect to any awards (internal or external) they have a chance to receive. "Some other managers might think I'm silly, getting up to nominate my employees all the time. But I am proud of the great work they do, and I think it's the least I can do for them." It is a terrific way for Rich to show them how proud he is of what they accomplish. The prospect of making others we respect feel proud of us is very motivating. It is not surprising that Rich's people have a strong sense of pride and ownership in their achievements since their extra efforts seldom go unnoticed.

PRIDE IN THE NUMBERS:
CELEBRATING THE RIGHT THINGS

Brian Williams is the site manager for Aetna's Tampa office. He motivates his frontline people differently from his direct reports. Prior to this job, he was involved in several turnaround situations in the health benefits administration field. When Brian joined Aetna four years ago, the company had just issued two lists—one of sites that would definitely remain open and another of sites that were definitely to be closed. Tampa was not on either list. Brian tried to eliminate confusion in people's minds with his response: "We're going to find out what measurements [determine] site performance, and we are going to exceed all expectations on every one of those measures."

Unfortunately, the uncertainty about Tampa's future had already hurt employee morale. In addition, there was widespread mistrust of past senior leaders, who were believed to have withheld information. So Brian committed himself to actively involve and communicate honestly with employees down to the front lines, using recognition and celebration to build pride around achievement. His dual emphasis on exceeding crucial performance measures and instilling pride brought Tampa through many of its tougher moments. The site was recently recognized as one of only six nationwide in Aetna's National Accounts organization for their record of superior quality and for achieving excellence on key performance metrics (e.g., lowest cost per member per month for any site in the region).

To his direct reports, Brian is a "real numbers guy," always working to make sure they stay current with the strategic and operating measures being emphasized by senior management. For example, in the past the metrics had tracked only production. Brian shifted that focus from pure production to include quality and customer service, which he believes also saves money that would otherwise be spent correcting mistakes. According to one of his direct reports, "He pushes us hard, saying that we're going to be number one or number two in the important categories." For the most part, these managers understand the priorities and the metrics they imply, and Brian uses those as the primary source of motivation for his managers.

For employees on the front line, however, Brian spends the majority of his efforts on creative recognition and celebration. Here, Brian is far more a cheerleader than a "numbers guy." His enthusiasm is as infectious as it is evident as he speaks in detail about the many different programs and the small, mostly nonmonetary incentives that engage front-line employees and make them proud to be part of the Tampa office. Many of the incentives are designed to reinforce performance on crucial business metrics. For example, he has established numerous trophies, pizza parties, and monthly newsletter features to recognize specific employees for such things as exceptional performance on quality measures, attention to detail, and pride in serving the customer. With programs that target performance, Brian tries to emphasize a broader context—to provide a meaningful "why" that lets employees know the origin and importance of priority measures.

Some of these originate as managerial, but others are peer-induced. For example, one program encourages employees to send notes of congratulations or "Gotcha's" to their peers (with a copy to managers), recognizing a job well done or positive feedback from customers. Recognition from peers, of course, is an excellent complement to Brian's managerial regimen of reinforcement. It enables employees to get actively involved in the celebration, as well as to interpret and better understand the office's strategic priorities.

Still other programs are aimed primarily at employee engagement. At the monthly "Breakfast with Brian" there is no agenda or time limit, and a small group of employees (different each month) have direct access to him as well as the opportunity to voice the concerns and issues that are most important to them. Here, Brian emphasizes the importance of letting employees know how he is following up on their suggestions. When an employee at one of his breakfasts talked about making the unit "a *worth* place, more than just a *work*place," Brian incorporated the idea and the language into further programs with his management team as well as in communications with all of his employees. Since then, they have explored the concept, solicited further input on how to make the Tampa office a better place to work, and taken actions to make beneficial changes—all of which makes employees feel proud that their inputs are valued and acted upon. Efforts to engage employees on a personal level provide an important counterbalance to the essential focus on performance, and Brian's employees respond with understandable pride: "Thank you for making me feel that you value us as people and not just numbers!"

To make sure that his programs are focused on the right behaviors, Brian incorporates language and messages from senior management. Recently, he started a new campaign to rally employees around providing quality and professionalism to constituents. Brian pointed employees to recent communications from Aetna's president and from the head of customer service, one on the need for professionalism with customers, the other encouraging employees to excel in their day-to-day actions. From these communications, Brian created a slogan as a rallying point: "Professional Results in Daily Efforts: Experience the Power of Tampa P.R.I.D.E.!" When Brian wants to convey messages to his employees about quality and service, he ties them back to this slogan, helping everyone to get motivated and aligned around issues that matter.

When asked if he is spending too much time with frivolous programs, Brian responds as you might expect: His foremost concern is with the numbers that drive his business, and he is convinced that his programs make measurable differences in those numbers. As quality has gone up, backlogs and rework have decreased, leading to real savings for the office. By recognizing his employees for their good work and creating an enjoyable work atmosphere, Brian has found that he can improve performance tangibly: "If you're reinforcing the right behaviors, then the reinforcement is almost always worth the cost." And Brian's frontline employees go out of their way to express their gratitude for his work, responding to each one of his programs with a flurry of thanks. "You believe in us and have nothing but encouraging words for all in your e-mails, etc. . . . You always demonstrate there is a light at the end of the tunnel and lead us there. You make me proud to say I work for Aetna."

Clearly, Brian's employees feel a great deal of pride in Tampa's performance. Although he always emphasizes Aetna priorities, his primary focus is on getting employees motivated to make Tampa a superior place to work.

MOTIVATION AT THE TOP

Brian Williams is an interesting case of a middle-management pride-builder who instinctively recognizes that he needs to motivate his front line with a different approach than what he uses for his direct reports. These differences can become even more pronounced at senior management levels of the company. The top levels of any organization are made up of people well schooled in the fundamentals of business economics, competitive dynamics, market share, and global positioning. Creating shareholder wealth, increasing earnings per share, and sustaining a rate of return that exceeds the cost of capital are terms and concepts with which they are familiar. Moreover, executives and upper-level leaders typically understand exactly what and how they are expected to contribute to those widely recognized enterprise performance factors—and how their specific responsibilities translate into individual performance expectations and opportunity. Their individual performance goals are typically stated in economic and market-share terms; these goals provide logical targets that motivate members of upper-level management.

At Aetna, for example, Rowe's turnaround effort started with a special task force effort to clarify a new strategic direction. The group consisted of several upper-level executives from different parts of the company. It was led by Tim Holt, the senior executive responsible for Aetna's large and profitable investment portfolio. This group worked for six months to analyze and pull together from earlier work a strategic direction that would guide the near-term turnaround efforts as well as set a course for the longer term. This work was reviewed with senior executives and a group of over one hundred upper-level managers in the company. It focused on what it would take to increase the company's return on capital, market position, and overall economic performance. These are meaningful factors for upper-level managers and serve that purpose well.

Their motivation is a function of that performance logic, and rational factors are critical. This is not to say that executives do not get emotionally charged up when they win a large contract or receive a big bonus. That emotion, however, has its roots in economic logic and rewards. The following paragraphs describe five rational factors that illustrate the motivations of most upper-level leaders and professionals:

1. *Economic gain:* Not too long ago, executives at most companies defined corporate strategy as "where and how to compete" to increase shareholder wealth. While the where and how dimensions still prevail, the best companies now focus equal attention on increasing eco-

nomic gains for customers and employees. A close corollary to shareholder wealth, of course, is executive wealth, since leaders who excel at increasing shareholder wealth are well compensated for their efforts. The connection between a company's economic success and the financial rewards for its top echelon is both rational and effective in motivating their behaviors. Certainly today, a number of top-performing companies define success in broader and longer-range terms. These companies also motivate their executives beyond shareholder wealth by emphasizing such achievements as customer loyalty and satisfaction, being the "employer of choice," and maintaining mutually beneficial partnerships and alliances. Nonetheless, the rational and economic components of those motivations typically overshadow any noneconomic results and emotional commitment.

2. *Return on capital:* This traditional metric answers the question "Is this business able to consistently earn more on the capital it employs than it costs to secure that capital?" Obviously, it is the fundamental financial imperative for business success over time. Successful investors, be they venture capitalists, merchant bankers, or Warren Buffet clones, have developed a keen eye for return-on-capital performance; and they make it the primary motivational element for the top management. Again, executive leaders who excel at delivering a high return to their investors are handsomely rewarded. Those who fall short on that measure are usually replaced.

3. *Power, position, and influence:* In politics and government, these factors are typically more important by far

than money or wealth. They are not, however, unimportant in the corporate world; in fact, it is hard to separate the motivational impact of power, position, and influence from that of economic gain. High-potential managers and professionals are motivated to climb the "ladder of success" (the corporate hierarchy) to achieve both money and power. And the higher up the corporate ladder leaders get, the more motivated they become by these two factors. At the extreme, their motives can sometimes be characterized by greed and domination. Obviously, these motivational forces work less well among the lower ranks simply because they are more elusive, less possible, and seldom realistic. Hence, while rational motivators at the top, they are virtually irrational within the frontline workforce.

4. *Market position and brand value:* An increasingly powerful and rational motivator for executives and leaders is the relative position of their particular business in the marketplace. In many companies, the value of the brand has become an integral if not dominating aspect of that position. In fact, the brand value of names like Coke, American Express, FedEx, and even Aetna sometimes exceeds the value of hard assets of the company. This was especially evident during the recent dotcom roller-coaster rides as well as the financial struggles at Aetna. Thus, the rational motivation to increase market position and brand value is relatively easy to convey among managerial and leadership ranks. Many companies will place those factors at the top of the "value chain" in defining the longer-term success of the enterprise. Moreover, when intense competitors like Coke

and Pepsi clash in the marketplace, emotions run high. Over the longer term, however, market position and brand value are basically rational motivators for executives in industries where those elements prevail. Of course, the value of a brand like Aetna can be equally powerful with frontline employees. "Aetna, I'm glad I met ya!" is almost as well-known today within major segments of employees as it was at the time it received heavy advertising support. Moreover, the phrase still evokes feelings of pride at Aetna that motivate many to improve service and responsiveness.

5. *Sustainable competitive advantage:* This phrase is perhaps the most widely accepted definition of a "winning strategy." Since most managers and executives learn about sustainable competitive advantage before they learn about any other element of leadership, it is hardly surprising to find it a primary motivator among executive leaders. It is not only highly rational, but also all-encompassing: You cannot expect to sustain a competitive advantage unless you attract talent that will provide superior value to customers who will pay a price that rewards investors at a higher rate of return than they can obtain elsewhere. While this concept is crystal clear to the leaders and managers in successful enterprises, it is not so clear among the frontline troops. It may be rational, but it is not particularly simple.

Admittedly, it is simplistic to argue that managers and executives are motivated by logic rather than emotion. Emotion plays a role in motivation at every level of an enterprise, as does logic. However, rational factors such as those summarized above are more likely to influence the managerial and executive ranks of a company for three reasons: (1) broad economic and market factors are more directly related to what upper-level managers are responsible for, (2) such factors are more clearly understandable in terms that relate to leadership training and experience, and (3) economic and market share gains are more directly related to what executives are paid. While these factors can be translated into terms that make sense to frontline employees, it is more difficult to keep that translation simple, relevant, and, most of all, emotionally engaging.

FRONTLINE MOTIVATION DIFFERS

We all know that life is different for people at the top than it is for the rest of the organization. The pay is different, the advancement aspirations are different, the personal growth ambitions are different, and the opportunities to excel are different. This is not to say that executives are immune to emotional appeals, or that they operate in a totally unemotional, robotic, "by the numbers" mode. The problem is that what is truly meaningful (and therefore pride-inducing) at the top tends to be less meaningful at the front line, either because of its relative complexity or because it is simply not seen as relevant to "what my job is." As a result, simple emotional factors drawn from local situations become more important to lower-level employees and actually tend to dominate among the highest-performing workers. A useful way to explain and understand these differences is to examine a half dozen or so common elements of enterprise success in terms that most employees would accept. The following illustrate how frontline employees perceive the six most common nonfinancial elements of enterprise success, namely, local reputation, product/service attributes, customer satisfaction, work group composition, peer approval, and competitive position.

1. *What do my friends and family think about my company (i.e., local reputation)?* Employees feel proud when people they respect want to learn more about their employer. I was reminded of this while doing research at the Johnson Space Center (NASA) in Houston, where a mid-level engineer was describing why she liked her job at the space center and what motivated her. Marie was obviously proud of her work on the space station, of being able to help our astronauts, and of having what she saw as a well-respected role in our society. Contrary to some of us who dread being asked about our jobs by strangers at cocktail parties, Marie relished having the chance to talk about her work. She never had to explain or justify why the space station was important, who the astronauts were, or even why she didn't make as much money as her contemporaries with other institutions. Moreover, people were instinctively interested in what she did and with whom she worked and were often a bit envious that their job didn't have the same characteristics of instant recognition and respect.

2. *What do people I know think about the products and services I work on (i.e., product/service attributes)?* For example, at Pfizer, one of the world's leading pharmaceutical drug manufacturers, people are both emotional and excited by being associated with Viagra and Lipitor. They really believe that they work on products that can

enrich lives and reduce human suffering. Somewhat surprisingly, this reaction is also true at Kentucky Fried Chicken, where employees are proud of what customers think about the chicken pieces and dinners they provide. Employees at General Motors are sometimes taken to customer shows to hear the reactions of people who buy and drive the cars they make. When one of the managers was able to get the particular truck model his people produced on display in the local airport, all of the employees felt proud, particularly when the comments of their friends and neighbors reflected favorably on parts of the truck that they had worked on. And they carried this message back to the plant floor.

3. *How do the customers whom I serve (personally or directly) regard the usefulness of what I do (i.e., customer satisfaction)?* Few things are more compelling to employees than direct, honest feedback from the customers they serve, be it internal or external. Frontline salespeople can, of course, obtain marketplace feedback easily—although sometimes, unfortunately, they become immune to it. Many nonsales employees, however, do not have ready access to their customers' views and reactions to their work. Making that kind of information readily available can be an important source of pride. At General Motors, for example, some plant managers make a point of sending several of their plant workers to sales and marketing product sessions with customers—primarily to ensure that the plant employees hear reactions to their work firsthand. Both positive and negative customer comments motivate those who go.

4. *Do I respect the skills, values, and work efforts of the people with whom I work most closely (i.e., work group composition)?* "Respect" in this sense is different from "like" or "enjoy," although in many cases there is a clear overlap. However, as I learned years ago from Dean Morton, former president of Hewlett-Packard, you don't have to like or socialize with one another to be an effective performance unit or team; you simply have to respect the skills, contributions, and work methods of your teammates. When Morton was describing some of the leadership teams that I was planning to research, he would often point out that the primary criteria in selecting each member of the group were complementary skills rather than personal characteristics. Others would worry that such groups "wouldn't get along," but Morton was confident that their mutual respect for one another's skills and experience would more than offset any personality differences. He was invariably right. Of course, personal trust often evolves from mutual respect as people do real work together; in fact, working together in an atmosphere of mutual respect is probably the most practical way to think about developing personal trust.

5. *Do people I work with and admire really respect what I do and how I try to do it (i.e., peer approval)?* To some extent, the "mirror-image" principle applies here: people tend to feel about you the same way that you feel about them. Hence, if you respect an individual for what he does or who he is, it is likely that he holds a similar degree of respect for you. Marvin Bower, the founder of McKinsey & Company, Inc., made a telling

comment in a meeting I attended as a new McKinsey associate over forty years ago that I still remember and believe: "We are not motivated by money, we are motivated by peer approval." And while McKinsey associates are not the same kind of workforce as NASA engineers or KFC franchisees, they do represent the "frontline" interface with McKinsey clients.

6. *Are we winning against the competition because of what I do (i.e., competitive position)?* The term *sustainable competitive advantage* is seldom used by lower-level employees, but they know the importance of winning against a tough competitor (external or internal). The management at KFC cultivates a lot of positive and constructive internal competition, because it recognizes the motivational impact of those activities. Mostly, that competition concerns how different internal groups are doing relative to key performance factors such as sales results or compliance with the Colonel's Dozen elements of quality chicken-meal service. Sometimes, however, the competition takes place in fun events where units compete against one another in sack races, relays, or other sports and games. Individuals and groups who "win" on the key performance factors are given conspicuous recognition and awards—most of which have little monetary value. An underground walkway at the KFC headquarters in St. Louis connects the headquarters offices with the technical center. It is called the Walk of Leaders and is filled with literally hundreds of pictures, awards, prizes, and other small items of recognition that people have taken great pride in winning.

While not comprehensive, this list is clearly indicative of the wide range of things that can produce pride within frontline employees and engage their emotional commitment to perform. Despite some obvious overlaps (e.g., winning against the competition or satisfying customers), it is usually a different list from the elements that motivate the top echelons of an organization. There also can be important differences within segments of the total company workforce or employee complement. What motivates a sales force will be very different from what motivates production-line workers or a technological group. And, of course, within large global enterprises, regional and cultural differences must be considered. What motivates employees in Indonesia can be very different from what motivates people in Germany—although it is likely that some kind of intrinsic or materialistic pride is at work everywhere. Nonetheless, understanding the differences between the top and the bottom remains the critical challenge, since what the top assumes about frontline motivation determines how the leadership system deals with both monetary and nonmonetary rewards for everyone.

FRONTLINE EMPLOYEES RESPOND TO INTRINSIC PRIDE

The most important difference between what motivates executives and what motivates the front line is the importance of intrinsic pride and emotional commitment. The front line responds more to intrinsic pride that engages their emotions. As I will discuss in the next chapter, enterprises that excel at engaging the emotions of their employees follow different paths to that end. But in each and every case, their leaders at many levels are masters at cultivating institution-building intrinsic pride—sometimes in conjunction with materialistic pride, sometimes not. Of course, they recognize that monetary compensation is important within any workforce; hence, they do their best to maintain competitive levels of pay. Seldom, however, do they aspire to be the highest-paying company in their industry. They pay enough to attract and retain good workers, but they rely much more on nonmonetary approaches to motivate key segments of their employees to excel in their jobs. A major reason, of course, is that they simply cannot afford to rely only on financial incentives without incurring a cost that will negate the competitive economics of their business model.

Some argue that stock ownership motivates employees just as much as it does senior executives, and perhaps it does. However, in the light of the recent volatile swings in formerly touted stocks, companies are increasingly and wisely wary of this form of employee incentive. In my opinion, the benefits of having workers own stock are more in recruiting and retaining them than in motivating them. In the first place, the value of any stock they own is difficult to relate to their individual performance. Daily—or annual—stock price changes seldom reflect what frontline employees do in their regular jobs, even at some of the high-flying enterprises such as Microsoft or Krispy Kreme. Moreover, the amount of stock owned by any individual employee is unlikely to be significant except for those in high-level executive positions. Frontline workers have a much more limited opportunity to benefit much beyond the point of partially funding their retirement nest egg.

Certainly, some companies, such as Microsoft and Southwest Airlines, note the number of employees who have become financially independent, if not wealthy, because of their ownership of company stock. Yet talking with such employees clearly reveals that the attractive wealth-accumulation opportunity does not motivate them in their daily work, even though it might have been an important factor in attracting them in the first place. They are much more motivated by the pride they take in their work, their products, and the reactions of their local customers, friends, and colleagues. In short, *money attracts and retains, whereas pride motivates!*

More interesting, perhaps, than what high-performing companies do is what high-performing managers and front-line supervisors do in average-performing companies. Such leaders seldom have much latitude in either what they pay their people or how much stock ownership they provide. Hence, they concentrate on engaging the emotions of employees by cultivating intrinsic pride in behaviors that link directly to enterprise performance. Strategic imperatives from on high are converted into "working visions" that have both rational and emotional meaning to workers. In the research we did for the book *Real Change Leaders*, we discovered that such working visions are often shaped by employees themselves.

For example, when the New York City Transit Authority effected dramatic changes in the cleanliness and functionality of the subway system in the mid-1980s, the working vision was simply "no graffiti." This was at a time when NYC subway cars were completely covered with everything from unreadable scrawls to bizarre street art and personal messages in a variety of languages. The graffiti mirrored many other aspects of the subway experience, which was not pleasant. A wise set of leaders realized that if employees could somehow clean up the graffiti, other elements of subway performance would also improve. For example, clean cars produce proud employees who improve levels of service that attract more customers and more revenue. You can be sure that this idea did not come from a high-priced public relations expert or some senior executive council. It was developed through the grass roots of normal worker interaction and supported by the more perceptive frontline supervisors and managers who recognized the potential symbolism of "no graffiti" in instilling pride to create a greatly improved workplace and more attractive form of city transportation.

Managers who are natural motivators in industrial plants invariably create interestingly diverse ways to measure accomplishment along with simple mechanisms that capture the attention and enthusiasm of the workers. These are usually consistent with the financial measures that investors, owners, and customers care about, but they are uniquely tailored to "connect" with worker emotions. Logic and economics matter, of course, but the real motivating power in these approaches comes from the emotional connection that often defies logic. There was no clear logic or economic value to "no graffiti," but it worked anyway.

Too many companies base their entire motivational approach for the workforce on the principle of "meeting (minimum) expectations," or what I call rational compliance. Simply put, this says to the worker, "If you do what is expected in your job, and the company remains competitive, you will be paid competitively; if you do not, you will be laid off." Of course, workers also hear the implicit logic, "Even if you do your job well, and the company runs into trouble, you may still be laid off." Rational compliance is usually based upon economic and operating numbers that shareholders and investors require; it seldom offers emotional or motivational meaning to frontline employees other than to raise anxieties about when and where the next round of lay-offs will strike. Hence, frontline leaders who are natural motivators of their people focus on what workers can really be proud of both individually and collectively, rather than what will or will not happen to them as a result of factors beyond their control. This is easier said than done, of course, and chapter 6 explores actual case examples of how different approaches by natural motivators have worked.

CHAPTER 5

■

INSTILLING PRIDE—PEAK PERFORMANCE ENVIRONMENTS

You don't have to be a student of management and motivation to notice the wide variation in the emotional commitment demonstrated by employees within different institutional settings. Walking through the halls and workrooms of most companies is an uneventful if not boring (sometimes depressing) experience; people go about their daily jobs in an unemotional, perfunctory manner. There is not much fun, energy, or productivity in evidence. *Dilbert,* the popular comic strip, captures the more humorous aspects of these common workplace environments, largely because of its ability to convert normal office drudgery and politics into laughable moments that most employees relate to easily. Most of the time, however, the only emotion evident within such environments is a gallows-type humor that reflects grim determination to "stick it out until something better comes along."

When you contrast these workforce emotions with the emotional exuberance that you find in high-energy organizations such as Southwest Airlines, Toyota, or NASA, the difference is striking. Moreover, that difference is reflected in the superior competitive results such emotionally committed groups obtain in both workplaces and marketplaces. Cultivating emotional commitment to perform is a motivational challenge that is best understood by exploring those organizations that have been able to sustain it among critical segments of their workforce over several years. In a recent book I described what we learned during a three-year study of twenty-five such enterprises. This chapter extracts some of the results of that research, particularly as it pertains to pride.[1]

As challenging as what peak performing companies do at the enterprise level to instill pride in employee performance is, however, the lessons from the study have a much broader usefulness at the individual manager level. In fact, it seems intuitively obvious that the best managers in any organization find ways to instill the kind of pride that spurs their people on to higher performance results for their part of the company—irrespective of overall enterprise performance. To understand this phenomenon, however, it is useful to recount briefly how emotional commitment to performance works at the enterprise level for those peak performers who have made it the core of their competitive advantage for several years.

UNDERSTANDING WHAT LINKS
MOTIVATION AND PRIDE

It is hardly insightful to point out that responsible companies strive to pay competitively, hire talent that matches critical work requirements, provide multiple advancement opportunities and skill training, set clear performance standards and goals, develop leaders at several levels, and reward the better

---

1. See *Peak Performance*. The research for this book was jointly sponsored by McKinsey & Company, Inc. and The Conference Board.

performers accordingly. These well-accepted and frequently practiced principles of "good people management" do not, however, explain the supercharged behavior of frontline employees in the peak performance companies we explored.

Emotional commitment requires something well beyond good human resources practices and managing by the numbers. A few examples from the Hills Pet Nutrition Company will help illustrate what peak performing workforces are really like.

PRIDE AND COMMITMENT

The power of frontline commitment at Hills Pet Nutrition was first promulgated by Peter Senge in *The Fifth Dimension*. I also was fortunate to be able to study the Hills Greenfield (newly designed) plant in Richmond, Indiana, during my work on *Peak Performance*. By then, the company was a well-known supplier of premium nutritional pet food for veterinarians, veterinary hospitals, and pet stores. While high-quality products remain a core element of Hills' continuing success, the unusual exuberance and commitment of its employees is what continues to make those products superior. It also explains the unusually strong relationships the company maintains with veterinarians. Hills employees at all levels are universally proud of their products, customers, and unique work environment.

That pride is instilled and cultivated by a set of processes and metrics that were essentially designed and monitored by the employees themselves. In fact, employee involvement is why Hills truly distinguishes itself from the many other companies that drive behaviors within a management-designed set of processes and metrics. The specific measures and work flows that determine behaviors at Hills may be no better than those of its competition. The motivational impact, however, is truly significant because of the obvious pride people at Hills take in the continual shaping and sharpening of "their" process. Thus, workers are fulfilled by their involvement in the process disciplines that enable them to perform for the enterprise. That balance between workforce fulfillment and enterprise performance is a continuing source of pride and employee commitment.

Of course, many companies can justifiably claim a clear set of metrics buttressed by well-designed processes or work flows. After all, managing by the numbers is the favorite watchword in most well-managed companies. Yet the employees of those companies have little to do with how required work flows are determined. Consequently, the best the company can hope for is rational compliance, e.g., "I will meet my quota or exceed it as it is reflected in my paycheck; I will not, however, become a rate buster just to make management's numbers look better." At Hills, the walls of the plants are covered with standards and targets that the employees have created and take great pride in exceeding. They actually have a "vision wall" where every employee has the opportunity to write a page on how he or she feels about the vision and values of the plant. Clearly, the attitudes and behaviors at the Hills Richmond plant reflect a lot more than rational compliance.

People are certainly paid well at Hills, but not appreciably more than the competitive norms. Interestingly, however, most everyone in the Richmond plant works at a skill and responsibility level that is one or two levels higher than his job title would indicate. For example, Debbie Carter told us that in her operations team leader role she actually functions as what would be a plant manager in most other workplaces. She also pointed out that many of the Richmond plant "technicians" (the Richmond term for employees) would qualify as supervisors elsewhere. Debbie and her colleagues obviously take much greater pride in the scope of the responsibilities and the impact of their working roles than they do in their formal positions or job titles. I believe that their intrinsic pride also keeps their focus on performance results rather than compensation levels.

Another excellent example of process as a source of both pride and value is found in the Hills Richmond recruiting process for staffing the start-up of the new plant, also created by the technicians. The process was designed to take recruits through a six-month screening to ensure that Hills would get the right kind of talent in the right places. Technicians who worked on the design of that process are proud of the caliber of people it yielded, just as those who made it through the process are proud of being selected. Initially, management argued against a process that would require six months to complete, but the workers convinced them that time was less important than talent. The motivational impact of this kind of involvement is hard to overstate: The technicians believed in what they were asked to do, worked hard at getting it designed right, and became relentlessly determined to make it succeed. If you don't think that reflects emotional commitment based upon pride of accomplishment, think again.

As we explored the approaches of the other twenty-plus peak-performing companies, it became clear that the Hills Pet Nutrition approach at Richmond for getting pride-based emotional commitment is not the only approach that works.

Each company applies its own unique formula to that end. At the same time, however, we did identify a few useful similarities among the outstandingly committed workforces. While these dimensions might be classified as common principles of good people management, the cases we explored practiced those principles with a good deal more discipline, focus, and consistency than is the case in the average organization. In every case studied we observed:

- *A disciplined balance between enterprise performance and employee fulfillment was enforced.* Leadership throughout the organization was equally rigorous and determined to bring about both enterprise performance and employee fulfillment. For example, at Hills the metrics measure levels of skill development and employee satisfaction as well as productivity, quality, and yield. As a result, the metrics of performance were matched by metrics and assessments of worker satisfaction, growth, and well-being. Hardly a surprise, of course, but the amount of attention such organizations devote to keeping these two factors in balance over time is unusual.

- *Rational compliance was simply never good enough.* Our case-study organizations were not satisfied with a workforce that simply "meets expectations." Instead, they are always "in hot pursuit" of the emotional commitment of the employees—above and beyond whatever level of rational compliance they might also benefit from. As a result, these organizations were typically much more aware of important differences between what produces emotional commitment among the employees and what is effective among the higher levels of management.

- *Institution-building (intrinsic) pride received more emphasis than money.* The leaders within our case studies did not place much emphasis on the monetary rewards for workers. And we found this to be true even in those enterprises where relatively high monetary earnings are a critical part of the motivational equation, such as investment banking, consulting, and entrepreneurial ventures. It was even more true among frontline, service-dependent organizations where the amount of money one can afford to pay is competitively limited.

- *Multiple sources of energy and pride were actively cultivated by the entire leadership system.* Recognizing that employees' emotions can have a powerful impact on their energy and motivation, leaders in all of our case examples drew upon more than one source for emotional energy and pride. In some cases, a dynamic top leader provided a source (e.g., Bernie Marcus of The Home Depot); in other cases, the energy emanated from a group of frontline role models (e.g., drill instructors in the USMC). In several cases, emotional energy was stimulated by a demanding set of customers (e.g., veterinarians at Hills Pet Nutrition); while, in still other cases, a primary source of pride was working with an intriguing group of colleagues (e.g., software junkies at Microsoft). The commonality among companies was not the source of the extra energy and pride, but rather that more than one source was carefully nourished and drawn upon over time.

- *Unique mechanisms and alignment approaches were required.* Emotional energy can come from activities that are fun, but not particularly productive. In fact, when you first wander through the work environments at places like KFC and Southwest Airlines, you wonder if all the frivolity is worth the apparent cost. Emotional energy feelings have a way of running away with themselves and can easily lead to diversionary and unproductive behaviors without appropriate alignment help. Thus, in every case we observed, it had become essential to design mechanisms and alignment approaches—such as the Colonel's Dozen at KFC or the Guest Satisfaction Index at Marriott—that would ensure behaviors that would benefit both company performance and employee fulfillment. Moreover, seldom were the same alignment mechanisms used by more than one organization. While in each plant situation a few key measures and disciplined processes ensure the consistent quality of the product, those measures also differ for each plant. Nonetheless, employees still take great pride in ensuring that the behaviors deliver the desired results. In each case, a few simple mechanisms had been designed to instill pride in the behaviors required for levels of performance.

Despite the importance of these basic principles for motivating performance, each company we studied applied and integrated them in different ways. And it is the "how" aspect of applying those principles that can be most useful for others because of the options represented. Our research identified five distinct and useful application patterns or paths—i.e., how to apply the above principles—that motivate higher-performing workforces in companies that have successfully cultivated emotional commitment over several years. Each of the five is very different from the others, but most of the enterprises we studied worked diligently to integrate one or two of the paths in ways that seem to ensure pride in performance over time. In other words, institution-building pride permeates and becomes the primary motivational force along each path.

THE FIVE PATHS

The name of each path suggests the particular sources of pride that are emphasized to engage the emotions of critical segments of the workforce. And to reemphasize, the underlying motivational force within each path is the *institution-building pride among the employees that sustains a higher level of emotional commitment to performance for the enterprise.*

Mission, Values, and Collective Pride (MVP)

Companies that excel along this path capitalize on rich histories of past accomplishments to lend credibility and motivational impetus to their current aspirations and values. They are typically described as "value-driven." Their leaders instill pride in a legacy of high performance explained by values that employees believe to be both distinctive and credible. People throughout these enterprises are openly proud of what has been accomplished by the enterprise, as well as how it has been achieved. While organizations with relatively short histories can succeed along this path, it is important for them to build credibility quickly among the critical groups of employees; otherwise, their motivation will not be sustainable when difficult times occur. The best examples of MVP performers have been through hard times. Employees along this path can be motivated by the company's intent to build upon its historical legacy, as long as the two are consistent and reinforcing. For example, when David Novak led the successful turnaround of KFC in the mid-1990s described earlier, he actually "resurrected" Colonel Sanders to enforce the consistency of his aspirations with the company's rich legacy of providing family chicken dinners of unique value.

The primary sources of pride along the MVP path may include a noble purpose (e.g., a major innovator such as 3M or a military defense force) or past heroes (former astronauts at NASA; Colonel Harland Sanders at KFC) or unique values (the USMC's "Do the right thing, in the right way, for the right reasons").

Process and Metrics (P&M)

Virtually every well-managed company presumes that it should excel at process and metrics control; it is a fundamental underpinning of any graduate business school education. It is hard to argue with the value of being disciplined about measuring the right things and maintaining effective processes for delivering value to customers. Often this is oversimplified as "managing by the numbers." Unfortunately, most companies are not disciplined about ensuring clarity and consistency of the numbers people focus on throughout the organization. Nor have their process designers been particularly tough-minded about ensuring process discipline and consistency where it counts for the customer. Nonetheless, everyone seems to recognize the importance of process and metrics, even if people don't know how to use it to instill pride and emotional commitment. Enterprises such as Hills Pet Nutrition that excel along the P&M path take the process and metrics doctrine one important step further: They insist that the technicians who will be measured against and guided by a particular set of processes and metrics are an active and integral part of designing those elements for the organization. Sounds simple enough, but it is pretty rare to find that principle in practice.

We found one of the better examples within the Avon manufacturing organization in both Morton Grove (Chicago) and Puerto Rico. Like Hills, the Avon plants have their walls plastered with charts and graphs that enable employees to track their progress on measures that matter to them. Not surprisingly, the Avon metrics and process are very different from those at the Hills Richmond plant. Interestingly, however, there are also significant differences between Avon's Morton Grove operation (which makes cosmetics) and Avon's Puerto Rico operation (which makes costume jewelry). But the fundamental principle of worker involvement in the measurement and tracking system produces the same kind of institution-building pride. This is seldom true with the "management by the numbers" systems that are followed in most corporations today, since the processes and metrics in those systems are created and installed with little worker input. Hence, rational compliance is the best they can hope for.

Entrepreneurial Spirit (ES)

Of course, the prospect of making a lot of money is an important element in entrepreneurial ventures, as is enduring a lot of pressure and personal risk. But most of those who excel along this path are much more motivated by the dream of creating a successful new enterprise than they are by adding another boat to their fishing dock or porch to their house.

While money attracts people to join entrepreneurial

ventures, the peak performers are also strongly motivated to succeed by the pride they feel in breaking new ground (e.g., the invention of new products, the commercialization of new ideas, and the design of new approaches and customer services). The Vail Ski School in Colorado is generally regarded as one of the best in the world. Ski enthusiasts of all shapes, sizes, and skills come from most parts of the world to learn from the best teachers and enjoy some of the most fun slopes in America. The school's ski instructors are actually individual entrepreneurs with their own "book of business," which consists of the skiing families who return to them year after year. Certainly, the instructors like the independence and economics of their job and savor the freedom it provides them. But what they take most pride in is the network of relationships they build up with their own customers. The turnover of instructors at Vail is less than 5 percent annually, unique in the skiing world, and the tenure per instructor typically extends beyond ten years. A good part of the explanation for that apparent loyalty goes well beyond what the instructors can earn; they are also highly motivated by the pride they feel in seeing their students develop and return each year. It is a great example of entrepreneurial pride.

I am sure that in the beginning, The Home Depot was a classic product of the Entrepreneurial Spirit path: high risk, high reward, and building a unique institution in the process. So it was with SWA and Microsoft, to mention the obvious. While it is true that such pride still permeates those enterprises, broad-based employee motivation is no longer grounded in high-risk, high-reward economic gains, because a smaller and smaller proportion of the employee complement can actually expect to be in a real "high risk/high reward" situation. When we studied The Home Depot the associates were motivated largely along two other paths: MVP (described above) and Individual Achievement.

Individual Achievement (IA)

For some time, I assumed that the Individual Achievement and the Entrepreneurial Spirit paths were one and the same because individual accomplishment is an important source of pride along both paths. As we worked through more cases, however, I realized that, unlike the Entrepreneurial Spirit path, the Individual Achievement path works well without a broad-based, high-risk/high-reward component for most employees.

Those who excel along the IA path view their individual performance and advancement (rather than team or collective performance) as their primary source of pride. Thus, the path requires creating lots of opportunities for individuals in critical skill categories to achieve and grow as individuals. Talented people, however, tend to leave such organizations whenever the "grass looks greener" elsewhere with respect to growth opportunity. Consulting, investment banking, and other professional service groups contain good examples of this path, and many of them suffered from the "grass is greener" phenomenon during the nineties, when e-commerce and the dotcom world seemed to have nothing but upside opportunity.

The story of the Post-it notes product line at 3M is a classic illustration of an environment that nourishes individual invention without the high-risk/high-reward prospects of a true entrepreneurial venture. Art Fry, the inventor of Post-it notes, is a typical hero among many 3M innovators. He grew up in small town in Iowa, where he began his education in a one-room schoolhouse. Following in his father's footsteps, he became a chemical engineer and started his over-thirty-five-year career at 3M while still a student. Art first thought of the idea of using a "weaker" adhesive for the Post-It notes during choir practice at his church. The place marks that he was using in his hymnal kept falling out between choir practices. So why not have a marker that one could stick in place for a reasonable time (but not permanently) without losing the marker or damaging the hymnal. It is the kind of idea that might occur to anyone, but only an environment like 3M would allow a naturally inventive mind like Art's to follow it through to product commercialization. And Art takes great pride in that he needed at least as much ingenuity to sell the Post-it idea as he needed to create it in the first place: "It was hard to sell the concept that people need a notepad that would sell for a premium price compared to ordinary scratch paper."

So Art sold it just as proudly as he created it in the first place. One year after the product was introduced in 1980, Post-it notes were named 3M's Outstanding New Product. If it were about the money rather than the pride of individual achievement, I doubt that Art Fry would still be at 3M, even though his promotions have elevated him to corporate scientist, the highest level on the technical side of the company. Invariably, we find that unless the Individual Achievement path is tightly integrated with one of the other paths, institution-building pride is difficult to sustain. This finding seems particularly important since too many companies overlook the self-serving aspects of an overemphasis on individual achievement. In 3M's case, that they excel along the MVP path provides an effective counterbalance for their individual achievers.

Recognition and Celebration (R&C)

The primary emphasis along the R&C path is on highly visible recognition events, celebrations, and hoopla. Walking through the plants, passageways, and office buildings of companies that excel along this path is suggestive of "a trip to Disneyland": People are usually laughing, pictures and awards of all kinds adorn the walls, and everyone appears to be having "fun on the job." At first glance, the more serious-minded executive would be convinced that most of this is a bit frivolous and costly, if not downright diversionary and wasteful. Further probing, however, reveals that the celebration and hoopla are an integral part of how these institutions instill pride in performance throughout the enterprise.

On one of my initial visits to Southwest Airlines, I encountered the preparations for the annual Halloween party, which is apparently one of the biggest celebrations of the year. The entire front grounds of the headquarters complex at Love Field in Dallas looked like a replica of Woodstock. Moreover, it also looked a bit extravagant to me, particularly since cost is a key performance factor at SWA (as well as a strategic imperative). When I commented about this apparent anomaly to my guide, Rita Bailey (then head of SWA University), she laughed and said, "Oh, the company doesn't pay that much for all this. Employees sponsor a variety of money-raising events during the year [such as car washes and bake sales] so they will be able to fund the kind of celebration they want." And they take a great deal of pride in doing it at virtually no cost to the company.

At KFC, I was invited to take a riverboat trip up the Mississippi River from St. Louis with one of the regional sales groups. The entire evening was consumed with fun and games, all of which were focused around widespread internal, constructive competition between the various sales and marketing units. Prizes and applause were bestowed on the winners, and every award invoked pride in one or more elements of competitive performance that was important for KFC. Moreover, the attendees were extremely energized by the evening; obviously, it was an important mechanism for motivating its frontline managers in an industry where large monetary rewards are simply not a realistic option.

Perhaps the most interesting testimony to the performance value of the KFC hoopla and celebrations came in a recent article in *Fast Company* entitled "Andy Pearson Finds Love."[2] As the article recounts, when Pearson was CEO of PepsiCo several years ago, he was named one of the ten toughest bosses in America. Now at Tricon (which was the Pepsi spin-off that contains KFC), Pearson has reportedly found a new way to lead, according to the article:

> . . . one based on personal humility and employee recognition. [At PepsiCo he] . . . fired the least productive 10 to 20 percent of his workforce every year. . . . These days, Pearson is focused on a different, more positive emotional agenda: "You say to yourself, if I could only unleash the power of everybody in the organization, instead of just a few people, what could we accomplish? We'd be a much better company." . . . At Tricon, David Novak [CEO] has established a culture that elevates the common worker in a way that brings out the emotional drive and commitment that is at the heart of good work. As a result . . . [Pearson] now recognizes emotion for what it is: the secret to a company's competitive edge.

Nonetheless, it is important to recognize this kind of recognition and celebration for what it is not, as well as what

2. "Andy Pearson Finds Love," *Fast Company,* August 2001, 78.

it is. In our case studies, we never found the R&C path to be effective on its own. In every successful company, the R&C path was complemented by excelling along another path, as well. For example, at KFC it is complemented by the Process and Metrics path, which it inherited partially from the Colonel and partially from PepsiCo. David Novak had the wisdom to combine the best of both. The same holds true at Marriott and SWA, where Mission, Values, and Collective Pride is a powerful companion path for Recognition & Celebration.

CONCLUSION

The five paths that lead to an emotionally committed workforce are impressive in their discipline, focus, and alignment. But the overriding commonality across all five is the institutional capability to instill pride that motivates higher levels of performance among large numbers of people. Companies that excel along one or two of these paths work hard at sustaining institution-building pride because they know it ensures them a long-term performance advantage over the competition. Moreover, it was clear from our work that a company that needs or desires to sustain an emotionally committed workforce is well advised to integrate two of the paths rather than be content to excel along only one (or to overload the system by pursuing more than two paths). And the secret to success is applying the discipline and focus required to sustain institution-building pride among those employees who make a competitive difference for you. At an enterprise level, this is clearly an ongoing challenge.

Of equal interest, and perhaps even broader value, however, is the question we are often asked: "Since my company doesn't appear to excel along any of these paths (and is unlikely to do so anytime soon), what can I as an individual manager or leader do in the meantime?" The final chapter is devoted to answering that question using the example of the General Motors Corporation, a landmark global corporation whose history and legacy of industry leadership are second to none, but whose tremendous size and global scope makes excelling along any of the five paths an almost insurmountable challenge.

CHAPTER 6

■

INSTILLING PRIDE — TRADITIONAL WORK ENVIRONMENTS

People within organizations like Southwest Airlines, 3M, and Marriott are highly motivated and emotionally committed to improve the performance of their business. By successfully pursuing one or more of the five peak performance paths, leaders in these companies cultivate work environments that are focused, disciplined, and consistently motivating for employees. And managers have the benefit of flexible leadership systems and mechanisms that enable them to tap into more than one source of emotional energy and to provide for disciplined attention to maintaining a dynamic balance between enterprise performance and worker fulfillment. Moreover, they have honed their managerial approaches to maintain and build that balance over several years. Thus, a leader at virtually any level in these companies can easily instill the kind of pride in performance that results in emotionally committed, highly motivated employees.

But what if you are not the beneficiary of that kind of work environment? What if your company is not in an attractive growth situation with a consistent history of winning in the marketplace and providing attractive returns to shareholders and employees? What if you struggle against advantaged competition, powerful union conflicts, global complexity, and technological disadvantages? What if, despite strong leadership efforts, your company is facing an erosion of its market position, product advantage, and employee capability? In short, what if you are a member of a well-established enterprise whose size, market position, and growth prospects are not very motivating for most employees? Obviously, motivation becomes a much greater challenge in such situations; and these circumstances are much more common than not throughout the industrialized world today. Managers in most large, global enterprises simply do not have the benefit of the integrated peak performance paths described in the previous chapter to help them motivate their people.

MOTIVATORS AT GENERAL MOTORS

The General Motors Corporation is a classic example of this kind of motivational challenge. It has been a leader in its field for over seventy-five years. Its history represents a remarkable legacy of leadership accomplishments starting with Alfred Sloan's famous model of large-scale decentralization. That model still stands alone as a unique organizational paradigm and has probably had more influence on corporations around the world than any other organizational design framework. Moreover, the company's achievement record has few equals, despite the severe competitive and union challenges it has faced in recent years.

GM remains a giant in the automotive industry and has been a pacesetter in global scaling (355,000 employees worldwide). Of course, the domestic automotive industry alone is huge, with the market spending on vehicles exceeding 4 percent of the GNP and the research efforts of the industry accounting for 10 percent of all corporate research and development spending. The company's several brands are legendary, and the UAW-GM Quality Network is perhaps the largest union/management partnership of its kind in the world. GM alone has created millions of jobs all over the world and seems to be a perpetual survivor of adversity—whether caused by governments, competitors, or unions.

Over the last fifteen years, "GM bashing" by the public, the investment community, and the press (plus the competitive inroads of foreign vehicles and the costly struggles to settle union conflicts fairly) has taken its toll. Because of the size and position of the union, the work environment at GM reflects years of conflict and compromise as well as partnership; it continues to evolve. It is a far cry from the days of perpetual conflict that culminated in the infamous Flint, Michigan, strike of 1937. Today, both management and union leaders realize that they must stand together behind quality products (as defined by the marketplace) if they are to continue to lead the global industry. The challenge ahead is every bit as significant as the journey behind. At a recent UAW-GM North America Quality Network conference in Chicago, the company's aspirations were described as follows:

1. Lead the continuing transformation of the automotive industry.

2. Reinvent the truly responsive multinational corporation.

3. Unify brand impact internally and externally.

4. Forge new levels of union/management cooperation and partnership.

These stated aspirations implicitly place a premium on motivating frontline workers through emotional commitment as well as rational compliance. Leaders at GM know that achieving this kind of motivation across their complex global business is extremely difficult. Nonetheless, they also know that the answer lies within the ranks of their better managers, who have already learned how to instill pride in performance during periods of adversity. Consequently, we decided to explore how some of them get it done. The GM Manufacturing Managers Council (MMC) helped us to identify and interview in depth twenty managers that members of the MMC consider outstanding motivators of their people. We also talked at length with the executives who nominated them and others who work with them—both union and supervisory. The results were revealing.

Case 1: A Leadership Partnership in Safety

On a bleak, wintry day in January, I arrived early at the GM Service Parts Organization (SPO) plant in Pontiac, Michigan, with my colleague in this research, Gus Vlak. Pontiac is in northwest suburban Detroit. To first-time visitors, the plant looks more like a large warehouse than a manufacturing facility. Clearly a model of industrial efficiency, its starkly crisp appearance added little warmth to what was a gloomy day. The Service Parts Organization facility in Pontiac receives, warehouses, repackages, and distributes parts for all GM divisions. Most of the parts are used by GM dealerships in after-sales and warranty service. Gus and I immediately noticed how clean this facility is—almost not like a plant at all. After watching the mandatory safety video required of all visitors, we sat for a while in a windowless waiting room.

In these rather uninspiring surroundings, we became infected with the enthusiasm and commitment of Paul McQuirter and Gary Lee Parker. In marked contrast to the bleak day, Paul and Gary Lee lit up the room with their positive attitude and energy. For two years now, Paul has managed the 937 employees and 1.8 million square feet of floor space that make up the Pontiac plant. Gary Lee is UAW 653 SPO Pontiac Shop Chairman.[1] He works in close partnership with Paul to create the positive work environment that has resulted in one of the best in terms of health and safety in the company (41 percent reduction in recordable injuries and time lost over the past two years). The plant's operating performance has been equally impressive.

Paul and Gary Lee take their joint leadership responsibilities seriously, and their mutual respect was clearly evident. I couldn't help but be reminded of the leadership partnerships I had found in the USMC, where platoons are jointly led by a strategically and tactically trained commissioned officer who is buttressed by a more experienced and battle-savvy gunnery sergeant. This unique combination provides the leadership capacity to motivate and care for each and every one of their troops, as well as to deliver more balanced decisions in battle. The same appears to be true with Paul and Gary Lee, who take as much pride in their complementary relationship as they do in their production accomplishments. In fact, Gary Lee's biggest concern was that Paul was about to be transferred to another plant, meaning his unknown successor would have to be integrated into the team. While this is not unusual within the GM management

---

1. The second-largest local union in the UAW.

system (the better managers move on quickly), it makes Gary Lee's role critical as the "glue" or provider of continuity across plant manager changes.

The pride that these two instill in their employees was evident at every turn in our plant tour. As Paul sees it, "the only thing that separates us from the mediocre is passion and pride" in what employees do and how they do it. He focuses his efforts around what he calls the "key three": vision, tools, and support. For him, it starts by getting the right people in the key leadership roles (people who "want to make a difference"). It always means making sure that people have all the tools they need to do their jobs, including training and appropriate skills. Paul believes that if the leaders cultivate an environment with aggressive goals and the necessary tools and support, then people will meet or exceed established expectations.

At the same time, both Paul and Gary Lee emphasize that "walking the talk" on the plant floor is what actually builds pride. Examples include such diverse things as recognizing the accomplishments of teams, supporting charitable events that are meaningful to the employees, and keeping everything about the facility clean and orderly all the time. They also believe that simple stories created about real people doing good things for the company strengthen the culture. In late 1999, prior to Paul's arrival, a bomb was found in the plant, and despite a $50,000 reward, no information surfaced on the perpetrator. Paul and his team took a strong position going forward: to create an environment where no one in the plant would ever consider bringing harm to another team member, and if for some reason a threat appeared, the person who created the threat would be apprehended "before the sun set."

That Paul and Gary Lee make safety the top priority is a strong source of pride—simply because it demonstrates concern and caring for the people. A recent article in the *New York Times* described how Paul O'Neill turned around Alcoa when he was CEO there prior to becoming the U.S. secretary of the treasury. Shortly after taking over as CEO, he announced that

> ...they weren't going to talk people into buying more aluminum and that they weren't going to raise prices so the only way to improve the company's fortunes was to lower its costs. And the only way to do that was with the cooperation of Alcoa's workers. And the only way to get that was to show them that you actually cared about them. And the only way to do that was actually to care about them. And the way to do that was to establish, as the first priority of Alcoa, the elimination of all job-related injuries. [Thus,] any executive who didn't make worker safety his personal fetish—a higher priority than profits—would be fired.[1]

O'Neill drove an impressive turnaround effort (Alcoa's profit went from $4.8 million in 1993 to $1.5 billion in 2000) around the simple, compelling theme of worker health and safety. Interestingly, but not surprisingly, O'Neill served on the GM board and became one of the primary advocates of getting GM leaders like McQuirter and Parker to make safety a primary theme in motivating higher performance. Much like the Alcoa story, Paul and Gary Lee's experience indicates that placing top priority on improving health and safety metrics instills both pride and trust in the leadership system. Safety also constitutes a "leading indicator" and determinant of future performance on other measures, as well. Members of the workforce see top attention being given

1. *The New York Times Magazine,* January 13, 2002, 24.

to something that really does matter to their personal well-being. Thus, it becomes easier for leaders to translate employee feelings of pride in improving safety records to anticipated feelings of pride in improving quality, productivity, and profitability.

Case 2: Process and Metrics That Instill Pride

John Buttermore was the manufacturing manager of the GM Vehicles Group and has been a part of the manufacturing leadership since the mid-1990s. He was recently named General Motors Corp. North America vice president for labor relations. We found his experience and his views on motivation at GM particularly insightful. He believes his early background in playing football (in the Navy and in the Special Operations) suited him well for his career at GM, which he views as primarily "a team sport and a people business." John was involved in a particularly critical period at GM when a small group of plant management veterans (the MMC) decided to do something about rekindling pride in both individual and company performance. It was a formidable task because of the negative external views of the company that had permeated the workforce.

By 1997, however, the top management of GM had created an environment that encouraged real change in the organization. The GM Board of Directors issued the challenge to the manufacturing organization to significantly improve the health and safety performance in the plants. The Manufacturing Manager Council, a small group of managers, took on the challenge and along with the UAW leadership made significant improvements. This can-do approach and tracking of key metrics was then expanded to other key manufacturing indicators of performance.

The original council of a dozen or so members has been expanded, but all were convinced that competing with the Japanese would require "something new" to motivate the workforce. According to John, "Americans like to keep score and Americans like to win. We needed a metric that would provide immediate feedback and rebuild a sense of pride at GM." They needed a tracking mechanism that could surface critical results and thereby instill pride in achieving higher and higher levels. Thus, a clear "scorecard" was developed and now serves as the primary measure of performance across nearly seventy different plants. It contains roughly the same measures for each plant, most of which are posted for the workforce in real time and are reviewed by the plant managers daily. The scorecard is grouped into five categories, as illustrated in the box below.

The same basic scorecard measures all plants. There is nothing particularly unique about this "balanced scorecard" approach; many manufacturing organizations utilize similar

> ### GM *Manufacturing Scorecard*
>
> 1. Safety (derived from Du Pont)
>   a. Loss workday case rate
>   b. Total recordables rate
> 2. People
>   a. Controllable absenteeism
>   b. Total absenteeism
>   c. Suggestion participation—days from suggestion to implementation
>   d. Training hours/employee
>   e. Communication

3. Quality (derived from Toyota)
   a. Direct run rate
   b. Direct run loss
   c. Shipping priority audit
   d. Warranty—incidents per thousands of months in service
   e. J. D. Powers tracking survey
4. Responsiveness
   a. Daily build to plan
   b. Vehicles in float
   c. OTD—lead time order received to leaving the plant
   d. OTD—lead time accuracy/predictability
5. Cost
   a. Actual labor hours per vehicle
   b. On roll hours per vehicle
   c. Nonscheduled overtime
   d. Total manufacturing cost per vehicle
   e. Budget performance
   f. Warranty cost per vehicle number of months in service

mechanisms. So why don't all such scorecards instill pride? First and most obviously because some managers use them to ensure compliance, rather than to instill pride. Thus, the metrics remain a control device rather than a source of emotional commitment. Gary Cowger, president of GM North America, sums it up well: "You can mandate mediocrity but you need to inspire excellence." The second and perhaps less obvious pride-builders' secret about using balanced scorecards is that they are selective: *they don't try to emphasize everything at once!* Instead they pick one or two central themes that are likely to be most meaningful to their people (e.g., safety or quality or customer service) and focus on or design a few compelling metrics (e.g., lost-time accidents or the Colonel's Dozen or Marriott's Guest Satisfaction Index). The really insightful pride-builders have discovered that the best way to get institution-building pride working for you is in simple, focused ways; whatever else may be required for balanced performance invariably "follows the lead."

The five categories on the GM scorecard were selected because they comprise what the MMC believes to be the main determinants of performance; they constitute a comprehensive framework. They are also natural sources of pride that insightful leaders can use to engage and motivate their people. For example, an emphasis on quality implies "we make products we can be proud of." The UAW leadership under Vice President Dick Shoemaker has been supportive of the quality improvement initiatives. Progress has been the result of this team's partnership. *Responsiveness* implies "we take pride in getting things done that matter to customers— in a timely way." *Cost* implies "we take pride in not wasting time or resources; and *people* implies "we take pride in how we treat and work with one another." Not every plant leader at GM sees the scorecard as a set of options to use to instill pride in performance, and many make the mistake of trying to do it all at once. The best pride-builders, however, are much more likely to get emotional commitment rather than rational compliance from their people—because they keep it simple and focused on what matters most to their people.

Most members of GM's MMC are strong believers in the value of pride as a motivating force, and their views are captured well in the following comments by John Butter-more: *"The number one driver in the performance of these plants is pride. . . .* Many of the people have a comfortable lifestyle not worrying about their next real meal and have less monetary incentive than other workforces."

In the minds of MMC members, the development of an overriding sense of pride beyond money is probably the most important source for improved performance.

Case 3: Giving All the Credit to Others

We asked the MMC members to identify individuals who they felt were among the best current plant managers at instilling pride in performance within their employees. With-out hesitation, Buttermore began with Amy Farmer, who is the plant manager of the Lansing, Michigan, vehicles plant. Amy has been in her current position for three years and manages approximately six thousand people. She has had an impressive record of success, including winning the J. D. Powers Plant of the Year award in 1997–98 for the Buick City Plant, which had already been earmarked for closing the year following her acceptance of the assignment. Even though the entire plant knew they were going to be shut down one year later, they still won the J. D. Powers award.

The Lansing Plant is close to eighty years old and has a long history within GM and in the community. It actually consists of two facilities: a body, paint, and interior-trim assembly facility (originally branded Fisher Body) and a final-assembly location (originally Oldsmobile). These facili-ties house fifty-three hundred hourly and five hundred salaried workers represented by two local union chapters; they produce approximately 450,000 cars per year. The workforce has achieved extraordinary results over the last several years, despite having the oldest facilities in the GM system. For example, the workforce

- Maintains the lowest labor hours per vehicle in North America in their competitive segment.

- Beat its budget targets in each of the last five years.

- Compiled a safety record of 0.2 lost workdays, which compares favorably with the Du Pont industry benchmark of 0.2.

- Won the bronze J. D. Powers award for the third-best plant in North America. The three car lines swept this category, placing first, second, and third.

These results helped influence the corporate decision to build a new plant in Lansing (the Grand River Cadillac plant). It is the first investment in a new assembly plant in the United States since Saturn twenty-four years ago and is tangible recognition that the workforce in Lansing is one of the best in the United States.

As Amy and her team describe it, "the difference is the people." Amy pursues a highly supportive and positive style of management to build pride among plant workers. She makes it clear to her people that achieving performance is not about personal gain for her, but about business results that benefit all. She goes overboard in giving credit to others but shoulders full blame for any problems. Amy's people describe her as "extremely bright, but not one to lord her intelligence over others. She doesn't micromanage, but she spends her time recognizing and rewarding others." Amy builds pride in each of her people by helping a number of them with their individual accomplishments and growth. For example, Jamie Hresko (who will be described in the next case) was the assistant plant manager working for Amy for several years and was an outstanding performer. She could have worked to keep him in that role and not tried to get him promoted, thereby reducing her own workload as well as delivering results that would continue to make her look good. Instead, she fought hard to get him promoted and moved to a plant that he could run himself.

Jamie's story illustrates how Amy works with her managers to help them grow and advance. It also has an indirect impact on pride in Amy's and Jamie's people. First, because Jamie's performance was well recognized and respected by the workers in Lansing, they took personal pride in his promotion: "He deserved it and we are proud that our efforts in his behalf helped make it happen." Second, and perhaps more obvious, Amy sent a proven pride-builder to work his magic in another GM location.

In the last year, Amy's plant workforce performed at outstanding levels against several critical dimensions of the scorecard. For example, her plant's safety record showed an improvement of 40 percent, thereby hitting an extremely demanding external benchmark. On responsiveness indicators, her plant achieved 100 percent daily built-to-plan, reduced the time it takes for an order to leave the plant to 6.2 days (versus a target of 9 days), and scored perfectly on predicting that lead time accurately for customers (which is hard to do). At the same time, her plant's score on nonscheduled overtime was 4.2 percent versus a target of 5 percent. And last but not least, the plant achieved an actual-labor-hours-per-vehicle score of 18 versus a target of 20—thus becoming the first U.S. plant ever to break through the twenty-hour barrier at GM (and perhaps across the domestic industry).

Whenever the plant and its people achieve extraordinary

results, Amy is quick to recognize and celebrate their success. Even as financial incentives have been cut back, Amy has searched out low-cost, economical ways to recognize, celebrate, and reward her plant and its workers. Simply put, Amy capitalizes on favorable metric results to build pride in and emotional commitment to performance across the workforce.

John Buttermore contrasts Amy's plant with others that do not perform as well, describing them as having a "victim mentality," i.e., their performance shortfalls are always caused by some uncontrollable factor (e.g., the product design is faulty or the plant equipment is old). Amy imbues her workforce with the opposite mind-set: "We can fight through anything." If there is a development opportunity for Amy, John believes it lies in modifying her leadership style to be a bit more forthcoming and outspoken. She is so supportive of others and so unwilling to take credit or extend her views beyond her people that the rest of the organization misses many opportunities to learn from her experience and leadership approach.

Case 4: Respecting What Went Before

Jamie Hresko joined GM in 1982 as part of the coop program at GMI (General Motors Institute). He worked at the Buick City plant in Flint, Michigan. The following briefly recounts Jamie's work history in his own words:

> I didn't come from a lot of money, and so I figured I'd have to work harder than everybody else. I tried really hard and they made me a maintenance supervisor first, then in production, then in chassis, and later a superintendent in body and fab, and then maintenance planning.
>
> In 1991 I joined the night shift at Orion [and] worked hard to change how things were done. . . . Then I got sent to

NUMMI[2] . . . where I had some authority to make change. I was made the assistant plant manager at Lansing Car Assembly. Then I was sent [back] here to Orion and promoted to plant manager. I've been here seven to eight months.[3]

Before our interview, Jamie took us to a team room in the plant. Some team leaders and an area manager had stayed after their shift to talk about the small-team concept Jamie had begun introducing as part of the GM lean manufacturing system. The following comments capture the high level of enthusiasm and pride in what they do and how they do it:

- "What's so great about this is you solve your own problems—nobody does it for you. . . . It's not easy—and I'm not saying that we're perfect yet, but we're fixing problems."

- "We used to have a float [cars taken off the line in need of repair before shipping] of fifteen hundred to two thousand cars; now we're down to forty to fifty on our worst day. . . . We do not require any overtime in final process. We are the lowest plant in North America for overtime use of this type."

- "Our J. D. Powers numbers are up [automotive industry measuring service]—we're not perfect yet, but we're edu-

2. GM's acronym for New United Motor Manufacturing Inc., an experimental joint effort with Toyota in Fremont, California. It was intended to help GM learn the "secret" of how Japanese companies could build better quality cars at significantly less cost.

3. Lansing Car Assembly is an older Oldsmobile plant that makes the N-Platform cars Pontiac Grand Am, Olds Alero, and Chevrolet Malibu. Orion Lake Car Assembly is an older GM plant that makes the Buick Le Sabre, the Buick Park Avenue, the Oldsmobile Aurora, and the Pontiac Bonneville, all large, "midlux" passenger automobiles.

cating each other; the people are engaged and empowered. It is a transformation—and I don't use that word lightly."

Jamie also introduced us to Lee Jones, the local union chairman; they obviously share a close working relationship. Lee described the importance of the effort, the improvements made, and how proud he was to be "working together with Jamie to make a difference here."

Later we took a plant tour during the start-up of the second shift. Jamie had been self-critical about not spending enough time on the night shift—"I don't spend as much time with them as I should, but I've got four little kids and I need to be home some, too." Nonetheless, Jamie knew many we saw by name and still had some close relationships from when he worked the night shift at this plant. He stopped to talk ice fishing with one man, kids with another, swap frustrations of the job with a woman. He jokes freely, trades banter, and takes as much as he dishes out. As a result, Jamie's people trust him and take obvious pride in working with him.

During our interview, Jamie shared some thoughts about how he instills pride in his people:

- My belief system [drives it]:
  —[I believe] the people can do anything—anything—if they understand what to do and how to do it. . . . First and foremost is consistency of message—I say the same thing over and over. Next—integrity. I [try to] tell it like it is. If I don't know, I say so. It's okay not to know everything all the time.
  —[Frontline] people are the nucleus and everyone else serves [those] on the line—trades, managers, me—everyone!

—Management's obligation is to teach—to lead by example. You'll often find me just jumping onto the line to fill a gap or contributing to a problem-solving session.

—[I also believe] you need to have a [personal] strategy, [e.g.,] what is your strategy with the union . . . [and] for engaging people? For instance, I have a [strategy for] . . . introducing small teams across the plant.

• Pride [that builds on the past]: My first task was to help people feel pride with what they'd accomplished before I got here. They were already good. Rich Conrad [plant manager] and George Johnson [production manager for the last nine years]—they're the ones who got this started. We've made some gains since I arrived, and maybe I had some small acceleration effect with the teams—but George and Rich were the guys and the people were the ones who did it. So I spent my first three months just reviewing what they've accomplished. I make a video every month so that everyone on all shifts gets the same message—"We've got a long way to go, but *look how far we've come!*"

—Senior management [always] wants to give credit to one person—the plant manager, whoever—but it's a process [that includes] a lot of people. Amy and I get a lot of credit for Lansing—but Jim Zubkas was there for ten years before us—he prepared the way—everyone respected Jim. He's retired now, teaching at the University of Michigan, something I'd like to do at that age.

• I [use] several sources of pride:

—Performance improvement—ten years ago this plant was horrible. Look where we are today. In the state-of-the-business videos every month, I use all the metrics—safety, quality, throughput, cost.

—Trust builds pride—people are proud that they can trust management, that their union and their management are working together—we have a code of "NO Surprises."

—I address the "rumor mill" in the monthly videos. The message is that if you don't hear it from me, suspect the truth of it. I will tell you first.

—We have a program we call Recognition vs. Reward. My managers and I try to send five recognitions a week to those we find "doing something right." It can be a simple "Thank you," verbal or written—like these cards I have.

- [Recognize the barriers to instilling pride.] Some old-line managers still don't get it. They think you have to beat it out of people. We [still] have way too much bureaucracy and politics. We're still too much "program of the month." Cost-cutting just needs to be a way of life.

  —But it's changing—I don't get discouraged, and I shield my people from some of the garbage they shouldn't see. And the biggest tool in my tool kit is *follow-up*. Somebody asks me to do something, it gets done.

In Jamie's mind, instilling pride in people comes from a lot of simple, straightforward stuff. Yet few managers take the time to master the pride-builder skills.

Case 5: Building Pride by Connecting to Community

The GM assembly facility in Ramos Arizpe, Mexico, includes both an engine and an assembly plant that produce the Buick Rendezvous and the Pontiac Aztec (among other vehicles). Hector De Hoyos Muñoz manages both facilities.

Hector started his career with General Motors when the

Ramos facility opened on April 28, 1980, a memorable date for him. The purpose of the new plants was to take production out of Mexico City, where the plants had a number of problems. In 1999, Hector became only the second native Mexican to lead the Ramos plant. His predecessor, who was also Mexican, had led the plant for less than one year.

The Ramos Arizpe facility under Hector's pride-building leadership has accomplished many impressive things, including:

- Achieved safety rates in the assembly plant that are twice those of Du Pont or Alcoa, the leading benchmarks for safety across all manufacturing industries.

- Operated for more than 10 million man-hours— fourteen months—without a single safety-related loss workday.

- Had more than 60 percent of all employees with perfect attendance last year, with a 98.6 percent average attendance for the workforce.

- Generated two legitimate suggestions per employee per year that created $8 million in savings in 2001.

- Launched the new 250 and 275 lines (the Aztec and the Rendezvous) three weeks ahead of schedule, achieving an immediate 86 percent direct run rate, which is higher than the ongoing run-rate average of the GM system of 75 percent, and operated accident-free for 378 days.

- Reached 80 percent uptime on the entire line and stayed there since November of 2001.

- Earned a global water management award for reducing the consumption of water in the production of cars from twenty-three to three liters.

Because of its location, Ramos Arizpe operates without many of the technological improvements found in other GM manufacturing facilities, e.g., few robots or sophisticated quality-measurement devices. Yet Ramos Arizpe consistently meets or exceeds quality and cost standards set by more technologically advanced plants.

Hector and his teams achieve these extraordinary results by unifying the workforce with three powerful sources of pride: individual learning, family economic standing, and belonging to a respected work team as well as the overall GM Ramos team. While employees are glad to be a part of the global GM corporation that provides jobs for them, they are more directly motivated by the three local sources of pride summarized below:

1. Workers at the Ramos Arizpe plant take pride in the skills they learn and values they acquire. Each new employee is involved in six to eight weeks of training when they join Ramos, and each employee has been exposed to a one-week off-site training course over the last seven months.

2. Workers also take pride in their ability to provide well for their families. General Motors pays very competitive wages in the region, which helps workers to raise the economic standing of their families. Families also know that GM will look after them in other ways. For example, GM offers workers without other transportation

free buses from nearby towns. Hector consistently reinforces the connection between GM and the families. Last year's Christmas party was held at a nearby fairground for twenty-two thousand people with toys for all of the children. In the summer, the plant hosts a day camp for wives, mothers, and children with educational activities including how to make toys and clothing, and day care for small children is provided. This is one of several ways that Hector reinforces the importance of learning and development within the family as well as at the workplace.

3. Finally, the performance of the individual working teams as well as being part of the "Winning Ramos Team" is a great source of pride. As Daniel Colunga, Hector's director of quality, puts it, "Pride is a big engine in how we do things at Ramos, and people understand how their own work affects the business." Or as Craig Johnson, another member of Hector's leadership team, puts it, "Nobody wants to be the weak link on the team."

Pride-builders make explicit connections with those things that people already feel pride about at Ramos Arizpe. Hector De Hoyes Muñoz has capitalized on what matters most to his people and built a community of pride based upon improving skills and team performance as well as the economic and social position of the extended family.

Case 6: Simple Themes to Overcome Extraordinary Obstacles

The Wilmington Car Assembly Plant was opened in 1947 to build the full-sized Pontiac. An impeccably restored model (vehicle number 20) sits on the plant floor for all employees and visitors to see. We are told that Wilmington has built cars for every major brand that General Motors has ever sold. As a result, plant workers more readily identify with Wilmington Car Assembly than with the global corporation.

Harvey G. Thomas is the manager of this plant, which now builds the Saturn LS midsized sedan. A remarkable person, he stands about six foot four, with gray hair and beard that were probably once blond. His plant office reflects the man, with flute and guitar music playing in the background, a portable fountain in one corner, aphorisms on the bulletin board ("Be a Learner, Not a Knower," "Be the Best"), and lots of live plants. Of particular note are the four old bonsai trees and two poinsettias (even though it is February). Harvey learned how to raise bonsai at a Zen monastery in Kyoto, and his first of these trees, a juniper, is now over thirty years old.

Harvey was raised on a Cherokee Indian reservation in Tennessee. His father, a full-blooded Cherokee, taught him about how people listen best to behavior: "Your behavior is so loud I can't concentrate on what you are saying." Harvey learned about leadership and the power of teams in the Army Special Forces (Green Berets) in Vietnam in the 1960s. He joined General Motors following his discharge and has worked in manufacturing management for twenty-five years. He describes himself as a "zealot about empowering aligned people."

Harvey and his assistant plant manager, Tyree Minner, manage a plant that consistently outperforms other comparable GM manufacturing plants on most metrics. To that end, they pursue a simple theme that encourages employees to focus on where each can "be the best":

- "This is the slogan of Wilmington." You see the signs and banners everywhere in the plant. "It's more than our slogan; it's a way of life. It's not just about quality; it's about how you live. Be the best husband and father; be the best at cutting your lawn; be the best line worker—it's all the same—it's in our blood." Obviously, a powerful source of pride.

- "We have a Be the Best Award—this award is given for solving a tough quality problem *every week*. Teams . . . present to both of us and our staff. We judge them on the problem, the solution, and how [well] they included everyone in the process. This is a cheap, printed cardboard plaque. I was initially embarrassed that we spent so little money on it. The frame is built out of pallet-strapping scrap. [Yet] people display it at their work site the week they win it. You'd think it was gold. We give the team a pizza party and videotape of them talking about how they worked together. . . . [All week long we] show the tape at the diagonal slice meetings [where attendees come together daily from all levels in the plant]. Last week the materials team leader came to all seven diagonal slice meetings. It's contagious."

Harvey and Tyree told us how this simple theme and the problem-solving continuous improvement mind-set originated:

- "In 1991 a GM official came here and said, 'We are going to close Wilmington in three years. There is nothing you can do to change this decision. Nothing you do will have any effect on it.' We have this on film. . . . We were building the Corsica and Beretta, which were also being built by other plants. . . . Our numbers were better, not much better, but better. The plant manager at the time waited till after the executive left and addressed the plant. We have this on film, too. He said, 'We may not be able to do anything about this decision, but we are going to make them feel really sorry that they made it. We are going to make them feel really stupid for closing this plant.'"

- "Well, he galvanized the workforce, quality went way up. These were not the best cars GM ever made, but dealers started asking for Wilmington cars. Throughput went way up. We became the obvious choice for a new model....So we got the Malibu launch run. [Again] they told us, 'It's only temporary—Wilmington is still closing.' The car had manufacturing engineering problems—you couldn't build it; we fixed them. We became the *obvious choice*. Now whenever we face adversity, we pull out the film and show it to the shifts; the part where [the GM executive] says, 'There is nothing you can do to change this decision,' gets a lot of laughs. We follow that up with 'Be the best.'"

As Harvey sums it up, "We always come through. Like I said, it's in our blood."

CONCLUSION: MOTIVATIONAL LESSONS

Clearly, the workaday world of General Motors is very different from the energized environments of the peak performers described in chapter 5. While the company has a great legacy going for it, GM managers cannot always draw upon companywide motivational environment. So managers within the GM system have to get creative.

First, they keep it simple. They use one or two focused themes, a few meaningful mechanisms, *and* continuous emphasis on local sources of pride that their people under-stand. Every pride-builder develops his own unique formula. Pride-builders connect to the workforce in whatever way they can: through pride in a legacy, pride in overcoming dif-ficult obstacles, pride in family, in the community, in work teams, or in role models. The bad news is that it is a lot harder to create emotional commitment to performance within a traditional environment. The good news—really good news—is that the better managers figure out how to do it, and they don't rely on monetary incentives. They can instill pride even when the production lines shut down and plants lose a product. The "motivators" at General Motors show us that you can instill pride in people in some unlikely, if not remarkably negative, circumstances. And that kind of motivational pride can make a huge difference in local and company performance results.

EPILOGUE

■

A LEARNABLE SKILL

may never be as "good" as Mom expected; but I still know what should make me feel proud, and I keep trying because I savor that feeling. I will certainly never be able to instill pride in my colleagues the way that Marvin Bower did; but I still try to follow his example. Thanks to Mom and Marvin, I know I can instill the feelings of institution-building pride in others—and thereby motivate them to higher levels of performance. I also know that few managers can expect to replicate the incredible pride-building talent of GM's Harvey Thomas as described at the end of the preceding chapter. Perhaps the remarkable Moms, Marvins, and Harveys we all know are born, not made. On the other hand, suppose we could capture 70 or 80 percent of what they do to instill pride and incorporate it into our own leadership approach. Clearly, we would develop a business performance capability well worth having.

David Thompson is a field measurement technician for Unocal, a leading petroleum company in the business of global exploration and production of oil. Dave is mostly self-motivated and certainly does not like underachievement in himself or his colleagues. His values and behavior set a standard of performance for others that is admirable and builds pride. His accomplishments are easy to measure. A few years ago, his commitment to excellence helped Unocal's Van Field in East Texas rise to a new level of achievement. Out of more than fifty oil and gas measurement audits conducted since the current measuring system was instituted, Van is one of only two North American production locations to have achieved the highest grade. The turnaround effort saw the Van Field improve the quality of the maintenance operation and, more important, change how employees think about measurement. Where before nobody had thought much about measuring production as a performance metric, accuracy in measurement became a key source of pride. At the heart of the change was the emergence of a true sense of pride in meeting, if not exceeding, the measures that Dave prescribed.

Part of what makes Dave an inspiration to colleagues is the integrity he brings to difficult work. Integrity is essential because a field measurement technician must determine the royalties given to the hundreds of lease owners in a field like Van. Since meters, like any mechanical or electrical device, can often fail in the middle of a month, Dave must estimate how much a lease owner should receive. As he points out, this is analogous to going to a gas station and getting five gallons of gasoline, but the pump stops recording at two and a half gallons. "Do you pay only for two and a half gallons? That wouldn't be right."

Dave was given the responsibility for the audit when he first became a field measurement technician in 1993. He approached the task with the intrinsic pride he always takes in his work and with the characteristic meticulousness that pride motivates. Since he knew little about gas measurement before this assignment, he had to start by scrutinizing the three-hundred-page field-measurement manual to understand every aspect of the process. With that brief introduction, he developed a few simple measurement practices that reached everyone from field technicians in the Gulf to revenue accountants in Sugar Land, Texas; and from clerical staff to operators and foremen in Van. Dave instilled in everyone a sense of the importance of measurement. He continually emphasized that measurement is really Unocal's "cash register," and accuracy is essential because the company is paid based on the amount of oil and gas calculated from the measurement meters.

It sounds fairly obvious now, but until Dave came on the scene, accurate measurement was not a priority. By Dave's second audit, however, the Van Field had progressed from a low grade to the equivalent of a B. And for the audit after that, they settled for nothing less than the top grade. Their accomplishment has instilled tremendous pride among the workers in Van, and Dave shows his pride in his colleagues when he says, "We have the best people in the industry right here in Van. You can send us anywhere and we can handle it." According to Unocal auditor Bob Faught, "The Van Field didn't merely improve, it was transformed by measurement," reflecting the commitment and pride that Dave was able to instill throughout the entire operation.

Much of Dave's success comes from the pride he takes in his meticulous attention to detail. Whatever the job, Dave pores over every detail and devours all background information before he begins. For example, as a school board member, he was well-known for never coming to a meeting unprepared. One of his fellow board members, Daniel Payne, describes it this way: "He wants to be invaluable. The more he knows, the more valuable he becomes." But note that his "value" in this case has nothing to do with monetary reward; it is entirely a function of feeling pride in his work and how others value that work in nonmonetary terms. It is the same kind of intrinsic pride Dave instills in doing things right for Unocal, its customers and employees, and the community.

These kinds of values, of course, start at home with mom, the family, and the community. Home for Dave is the town of Van, population 1,854, located in the lush greenery of East Texas. Since the discovery of oil in Van on October 14, 1929, oil and gas exploration and production have played a central role in the life of the community. Over four hundred pumping units are located throughout the town; Unocal is a part of the community's social and economic fabric. "Unocal workers have a sense of ownership in all town events," says Dave. "This town and [its] celebrations are about us." And Dave and his colleagues take great pride in maintaining that connection. Even though the number of Unocal employees in Van has declined over the years, the strong presence of its retirees keeps Unocal's history at the forefront of people's minds. Frequent office and field visits by some of the retirees ensure that the tradition of excellence is passed on through people like Dave.

In the over twenty-five years that Dave Thompson has worked at Unocal, he has captured the spirit of the company as well as the respect of his friends and neighbors in Van. He is valued not just for the work he does every day, but for the pride and relentless pursuit of excellence and integrity that he seems to instill in everyone he works with both on the job and in the community. "People like Dave are contagious," says Dave's auditing colleague and friend Bob Faught. "Others see and feed off of his attitude, success, and the pride he takes in doing the job right." Dave is an instinctive pride-builder based upon his personal values with respect to excellence, integrity, and company performance.

But the Dave Thompsons of this world become instinctive pride-builders long before they join the corporate world. Hence, employers cannot expect to teach their employees or managers to "be like Dave," and an important part of Dave's makeup is well beyond what Unocal can control or even influence. But that doesn't mean that Unocal's only choice for instilling institution-building pride among its employees is to "find more Daves." We may never develop a cadre of hundreds of Dave Thompsons whose pride in their work drives them to the highest levels of performance. We can, however, expect to get dozens more (perhaps even hundreds) of "eighty percenters," who learn both the importance of institution-building pride and how to instill it in the people they work with. Certainly, if we can teach "managing by the numbers" to lots of well-intentioned potential managers, we can also develop useful mechanisms and techniques for helping them get better at instilling institution-building pride.

Instilling pride can be viewed as an investment in motivation for an organization because the benefits recur over time. This is particularly true where the leadership system incorporates multiple sources of pride and provides mechanisms to encourage frontline leaders to develop their own pride-building skills. While such investments are not trivial, they frequently are one of the least expensive ways for an organization to improve its performance because they create pride-builders throughout the company who retain their effectiveness over time.

As the case examples and commentary throughout this book illustrate, there are many potential sources of pride—and many approaches, tools, and mechanisms that the better pride-builders use to instill pride that motivates business performance. Unfortunately, we found no one magic formula or specific set of tricks that fits every situation. Hopefully by now, however, most readers have already identified ways to strengthen their own pride-building capability. To further your exploration of how you might get better at instilling institution-building pride among your colleagues, this chapter concludes with a "starter list" of learnable techniques that emerged from our research.

A STARTER LIST TO ENCOURAGE PRIDE-BUILDERS

As we pursued our research with "workplace motivators" in tough, traditional work environments such as General Motors, Unocal, Aetna, and elsewhere, we gained some valuable insights to go along with what we learned from the peak performance environments. The most valuable insight, of course, is that you do not have to work for one of the peak performance companies to instill pride among your colleagues and associates. Intrinsic, institution-building pride motivates people in almost any environment, and we found it to be just as powerful within the workforces of companies facing severe performance difficulties.

We also found that the best "manager motivators" concentrate their efforts along three fundamental themes: (1) always have your compass set on pride (don't mistake pride in the destination for pride along the journey), (2) localize as much as possible (don't wait for the company or its senior leaders to instill it), and (3) integrate multiple sources of pride around a few simple messages (don't confuse your people with needless complexity). And then, try to avoid the obvious pitfalls (don't assume you can follow the path instinctively). These starter ideas can apply to individual pride-builders as well as to organizations that seek to encourage them.

Always Have Your Compass Set on Pride

Where motivation is concerned, the journey is more important than the destination. Pride-builders recognize that instilling pride along the way is the only way to keep pride in the destination in focus. Thus, it is more important for people to be proud of what they are doing every day than it is for them to be proud of reaching their destination. And, of course, the best pride-builders consistently ignore money in their efforts to motivate high levels of performance. Their primary focus is on emotional appeals, i.e., how people will feel when they achieve more than expected results that matter for themselves as well as the company. Pride-builders are always in hot pursuit of emotional commitment rather than rational compliance; that is why their compass always points to pride. Four specific techniques are worth mentioning in this context:

1. *Clarify exactly what matters and why it matters.* Employees need to understand what is important about their jobs and why it matters to excel at the little things as well as the big ones. The "working visions" that real change leaders employ invariably touch people's emotions as well as capturing compelling images of the destinations being pursued. When the New York City Transit Authority effort coined the term *no graffiti,* no one had to speculate about what it meant or why it mattered. It was a working vision that brilliantly captured

what success would look like both at the end and along the way.

2. *Stimulate people's memories, both real and vicarious.* Since people can seldom feel the pride of completion at the beginning of a difficult journey, it is critical for them to remember what it will feel like. Recalling their own experience along earlier successful journeys, or vicariously relating to the analogous experiences of others they know about, can be very motivating. The sixteen Warrior Stations in the Crucible part of the USMC's boot camp is a good example of building pride in recruits who have yet to experience battlefield pride. Peter Senge once reminded me that if you have ever been a member of a true high-performance team, you will probably spend the rest of your life searching for another one. And most of us can vicariously recall team feelings of pride when we watch a movie like *The Dirty Dozen*. Pride-builders use both real and vicarious techniques of recall to great advantage.

3. *Celebrate the "steps" as much as the "landings."* You need to instill pride in the little things—one step at a time—as well as in the major accomplishments. Tom Peters and Robert Waterman reminded us all of the importance of "early wins" in achieving "excellence." Celebrating an early, seemingly insignificant "win" has the same effect on adults as does cooking and eating that first fish your daughter catches—or going bonkers the first time your dog poops on the paper! Pride-builders are masters at spotting the small achievements that will instill pride in their people, and making an

appropriate fuss over each and every one—just as your mom did when you screwed up the last line in your first school play and unintentionally brought down the house with laughter.

4. *Focus on "containers" that are never empty/never full.* Michael Jordan and Tiger Woods are super sports examples of this philosophy. Neither of them is ever content with a victory that most of us would regard as "the ultimate dream." Conversely, neither of them ever sees a loss as something to fret over. Marvin Bower still takes great pride in the accomplishments of McKinsey & Company, Inc., but his high expectations for that firm will never be completely satisfied, despite McKinsey's continuing global leadership in its field and enviable influence with prestigious clients. The pride-builders keep a continual improvement aspiration front and center for themselves and their people; it is why the journey usually receives more focus than the destination. The pride-builders are also remarkably able to rise out of the ashes of disaster to motivate their troops. No catastrophe is devoid of pride potential. Even during the low period of press and public attacks on GM and Aetna, their pride-builders were able to instill pride in what their company was doing and could become.

Localize as Much as Possible

Despite the impressive leadership systems in the peak-performance organizations, we have discovered that the best efforts are localized. They stem from frontline managers who know their people, their market situation, and the practical realities of their work environment. These local sources of pride provide the kind of flexibility to adapt that is so critical over time.

But what works at one locale may not work at another. One of the best motivators we interviewed at GM was Rick Sutton, who was then manager of a GM Powertrain plant in Saginaw, Michigan. He had come from a three-year stint at another GM plant in Massena, New York, which was half the size of the Saginaw facility. At Massena, Rick readily got to know the employees individually and got them to trust him personally. Personal relationships were the key to instilling pride at the Massena plant. When he transferred to the larger Saginaw Powertrain plant, however, he found he could no longer rely on individual personal relationships. In Massena, he had physically moved his office into the middle of the plant floor where he was clearly visible and accessible to everyone. If he were do to that in his current situation, he would be completely swamped. Hence, he has resorted to more delegation, a monthly video communication, and other methods of instilling pride.

Rick makes the point that videos and other nonpersonal communications can be counterproductive in developing trust and relationships. "Videos in this context are only good for one thing, and that is getting the same information to a very large group of people at the same time, giving the first-level managers a tool to deliver a common message. Videos are a stopgap only. I have a regular schedule to personally visit these teams that are viewing these videos [forty teams per year!]. I go to their shift at their regular meeting time. Also, in each video there is a personal encouragement to any teams that are not on the current schedule or have pressing needs or issues to invite me to their meeting, anytime, any day. This behavior, which duplicates the easy availability that I had in Massena, is what really develops the relationship, trust, and instills a sense of pride."

Using his leadership team to leverage his efforts became much more critical in the larger facility. What instills pride in one worker does not necessarily work for others, and unless you have either a personal relationship with each worker (or a leadership system that connects with all workers), you will leave many by the wayside. A few techniques that were highlighted in earlier examples are also worth repeating here:

1. ***Draw primarily on local analogies and role models.*** If you have ever watched the Special Olympics on television (or been fortunate enough to attend in person), you see marvelous examples of people taking pride in the achievements of others who like themselves have totally forgotten their disabilities for the day. Various event winners, of course, are proud of their victory, but as much or more pride is on the faces of those who simply finish their event. Everyone who competes is a winner, and the local role models abound. This kind of athletic pride has nothing to do with Michael Jordan or Tiger Woods. It is all about those who come to try and try again. They are the heroes and role models that matter here. The same is true in the corporate world. The most meaningful role models and pride-inspiring heroes are local—such as Dave Thompson at Unocal and Amy Farmer at GM. You need look no further than your own work groups, and you certainly need not search very far up the hierarchy.

2. ***Tap into family, community, and union events.*** Pride-builders invariably go outside the workplace to find

sources of pride that will be relevant to the workplace. Almost every frontline "motivator" we have observed taps into more than one source of pride in a disciplined way. Often these sources include activities involving family, union ties, and community service. Jamie Hresko's view is typical of managers who integrate outside pride sources with the work environment, e.g.:

- "Community service builds pride. I sponsored a Big Brother and Big Sister program in Lansing. Here, it is Scouting [that] people feel good about—that we are helping the community, and that they [personally] are helping."

- "We sent two cars to the Fire Department of New York City. We had a shipping ceremony where everyone turned out to send the cars."

- "Events build pride, like the day at the plant for Big Brothers and Sisters, the Make a Wish Run."

And if your workplace is unionized, involvement in union events and issues is crucial. The best pride-builders really do "partner" with their local union leaders; seldom are major decisions and actions taken that do not reflect the approval and support of the appropriate union representatives.

3. *Trigger the "anticipation" of feeling proud locally.* Clearly, the Marines are proud of the Corps and the many battles they have won for the USA. But the looks of pride on their faces during the rigorous events at boot camp have a lot more to do with what is happening locally than it does with anything that happened in Vietnam. When you are trying to instill pride in future performance, it is much easier to get your people to

anticipate those motivation feelings by drawing upon stories and heroes that are local and well-known to your people. Triggering feelings of pride that must anticipate future performance is easier to do when the trigger mechanisms are familiar and credible.

Integrate around a Few Simple Themes

The more diverse the activities, however, the more important it is to have two or three themes that tie it all together. In Jamie's case, he focuses on telling it like it is, convincing his people they can do anything, partnering with the union, and dispensing credit liberally. A couple of other techniques that we encountered are worth mentioning here:

1. *Develop and repeat your most compelling stories.* People seldom tire of good stories that stir up feelings of pride. As we emphasized earlier, pride-builders find ways to stimulate people's memories of and empathy for feeling proud. Meaningful stories are an excellent way to accomplish this. A good story for motivational purposes is one that is honest; it recognizes imperfections and mistakes. A good story also uses real names, places, and facts; it is not a fanciful fabrication of someone's imagination or wishful thinking. And last but not least, a good story makes a few points clearly; it is neither complicated nor comprehensive. In 1995, Howard Gardner wrote a landmark book entitled *Leading Minds: An Anatomy of Leadership,* in which he explored the attributes and approaches of ten truly great world leaders ranging from Margaret Mead to Mahatma Gandhi. One of the most intriguing findings of his work was that "whether direct or indirect, lead-

ers fashion stories—principally stories of identity. It is important that a leader be a good storyteller, but equally crucial that the leader embody that story in his or her life. . . . When the leader is dealing with a diverse, heterogeneous group, the story must be sufficiently elemental to be understood by the untutored, or 'unschooled' mind."[1] While Gardner's work is focused on leaders of incredible stature, his finding about the value of compelling stories is certainly applicable to the stories that pride-builders tell.

2. *Seek out "leading indicators" to simplify and sequence your task.* Well-intended managers and leaders have a natural tendency to pursue comprehensive frameworks. We like to be sure that we are covering all the bases, and that we are covering them virtually simultaneously. Speed and complexity are forces that every manager and leader is increasingly wrestling with, so it is no wonder that such frameworks evolve and serve their purpose within executive circles. At the front line, however, we have to continue to pay attention to Tom Peters's timeless advice: "Keep it simple, stupid." A bit harsh, perhaps, but worthy of reprise here.

When confronted with a comprehensive framework designed by some consultant and promulgated by top management, the pride-builder invariably "cuts it down to size." If several metrics and priorities are involved, the pride-builder will pick one or two to emphasize for his people. If he can find a "leading indicator," as McQuirter and O'Neill did with safety at GM and

---

1. Howard Gardner, *Leading Minds: An Anatomy of Leadership* (New York: Basic Books, a Division of Harper Collins, 1996), ix.

Alcoa, he will make that his driving focal point. Even new priorities, such as measurement accuracy for Unocal in Van, Texas, can be powerful focal points. If not, the pride-builder will find a way to sequence the framework so that those people he needs to motivate are not overwhelmed or confused—and so the compass remains set on the primary source of pride.

Avoid the Common Pitfalls

Most of the pitfalls of "pride eroders" are well-known, yet managers consistently stumble into them. Ignore them at your peril if pride in performance is your goal. For example, we all know that unions have legitimate interests and concerns that are not always aligned with company performance aspirations. Yet few frontline managers involve union leaders in ways that increase the alignment, demonstrate trust, and build pride in performance. Gary Lee Parker was a true leadership partner with Paul McQuirter. He was included in every important decision and was critical to the resolution of most key issues. We didn't specifically ask that Gary Lee be included in our interview with Paul, but Paul wouldn't have done it any other way.

The planned rapid rotation of leaders who are on the "fast track" is characteristic of many companies, yet few seem to recognize the negative impact of this kind of rotation on the motivation, trust, and commitment of the workers. We assume that everyone understands that is how high-potential managers are rewarded. Yet without some consistent continuity across these leadership transitions, the pride that one leader instills can be lost. A strong partnership like Gary Lee and Paul's can help. And an aligned leadership team that remains at the helm during the transition can also make a huge difference. Some years ago, I was researching an effective leadership team at Hewlett-Packard. Because of the business unit's high performance with this team, the general manager was promoted. Despite his strong recommendation that one of his team assume his vacated role, management brought in a new leader. It took the unit eighteen months to rebuild the trust and pride lost from this all-too-common senior leadership decision.

Equally frustrating is the across-the-board enforcement of top-down methodologies or arbitrary insistence on "consistency" across diverse units, which actually constrains local flexibility. While a clear vision and strategy are essential, and alignment frameworks can help, leadership mandates that overly inhibit local initiative and flexibility are likely to work against balanced pride over time. Even focused performance metrics require local interpretation and adjustment to fit the realities of different competitive situations and work environments. Southwest Airlines is tightfisted about costs, since its success is based upon a low-cost strategy that is contingent on the behavior of every employee. Yet Colleen Barrett (and Herb Kelleher before her) does not tell employees what to spend and what not to spend. In fact, their Halloween celebration would make a strong financial controller nervous— until he realized that the employees themselves (on their own time) raise all the money for their favorite event.

A common pitfall, of course, is simply overreliance on monetary incentives. It is the most common roadblock to intrinsic pride because it focuses the employee on materialistic indicators. We have gradually learned the hard way that the time-honored focus on stock ownership as a primary motivational tool works only when things are rosy. When the ship hits rough waters, stock values only distract the broad base of employees. Those who believe that stock ownership is the answer to keeping the employee aligned with enterprise performance are missing more than half of the equation. What workers do in their everyday jobs seldom reflects itself directly in stock performance. Moreover, assuming that somehow the entrepreneurial spirit of ownership will prevail through the stock in an enterprise of any size is truly naive. While compensation and stock opportunity can provide important "attraction and retention" value, you need to look well beyond financial incentives to take advantage of the motivational power of pride.

Perhaps the worst pitfall is the one to conclude on: complexity. Don't overload the system! Because institution-building pride comes from many sources and utilizes many mechanisms, it is all too easy to try to do it all at once. This seldom works for long for three basic reasons: (1) unintended contradictions easily creep into your messages and programs; such contradictions erode pride and weaken motivation; (2) employees need to work within their capacity to achieve results that they can easily understand and explain to friends and family; an overloaded system based upon a comprehensive framework makes this virtually impossible; and (3) pride comes from "excellence" in something, however defined, rather than incremental increases along a modest incline.

CONCLUSION

Pride is a powerful motivating force. As the title of this book suggests, I believe it is the greatest motivational force in the world. Of course, if its definition includes both self-serving and institution-building pride, the force includes both positive and negative forms of motivation. For leaders in companies that need to motivate their people to achieve challenging aspirations and increasing levels of performance relative to the competition, the challenge is getting pride that leads to more good than bad results. This is much easier said than done, particularly if the focus is primarily on monetary incentives or individual egos.

Obviously, I believe strongly that instilling pride—institution-building pride—can be a powerful, positive performance motivator. Moreover, just as classic performance management skills and techniques can be learned and institutionalized, so can the ability to instill institution-building pride in the workforce. Perhaps the best image for me of what the game of pride-building is all about occurred during one of my visits with the Marines at Parris Island. I was conducting an informal discussion with a small group of recruits who were a couple of weeks away from their graduation. One of the recruits was a young woman named Amy (although recruits can't use their first names at Parris Island), who probably weighed no more than one hundred pounds dripping wet, and whose demeanor was quiet and modest. She clearly seemed like a potential "misfit" to me, based on my notion of the tough, battle-hardened veterans she was presumably trying to emulate. Unable to contain my curiosity, I asked Amy why she wanted to become a Marine. Her answer reflected her ten weeks of Parris Island value-shaping and pride-building, as well as her potential as a future Marine. She pondered my question briefly, and as her eyes literally sparkled and her whole face lit up with pride, she said simply and convincingly, "Mr. Katzenbach, the Marines make me shine!" As she elaborated, it became clear that Amy meant that over the past ten weeks she had discovered that she was capable of so much more than she had ever imagined—and her pride in that discovery would continue to motivate her throughout her life. Perhaps this simple story is the most compelling way to illustrate the power of institution-building pride.

ACKNOWLEDGMENTS

M ost important, I must acknowledge the serious readers of *Peak Performance,* many of whom stimulated me to write this book by persistently asking me a difficult question: What do you do if the company you work for is not like one of your peak performers, but you still need emotional commitment from the people who work with you? That question more than anything else led me to delve into the magic of the pride-builders in more traditional work environments. It was there that I rediscovered the motivational power of pride, hardly a secret to top performers in any field of endeavor. And in returning to the research base behind *Peak Performance,* it was easy to see the common thread of institution-building pride that permeates each of the five paths. What was less apparent, however, was the importance of pride as a primary source of motivation in companies whose work environments are not a natural source of pride, or where difficult circumstances threaten the growth, profitability, and competitive effectiveness of the enterprise.

Hence, I am also indebted to the dozens of pride-builders, many of whom are featured in this book, as well as their leaders who supported our case work within more challenging work environments. Most deserving of special mention is Jay Wilber of General Motors Corporation. Almost from the beginning, Jay took a very personal interest in this work and was able to convince Troy Clarke and other respected members of GM's North American Manufacturing Managers Council to help us identify and learn from the experiences of some of the best motivators in the company. In a similar vein, I deeply appreciate the cooperation and support of John W. Rowe, M.D., and Ronald A. Williams (CEO and COO respectively) of Aetna and the pride-builders in their organization whose cases were instrumental in helping us understand how pride works during troubled times.

In addition, many people helped us shape and test our emerging conclusions and clarify the lessons to be learned. My partners, Marc Feigen, Niko Canner, and Kenny Kurtzman, not only participated in important aspects of the case work, but also generously provided critical commentary and research staff support. Alan Culler led our research at General Motors, Rusty O'Kelley at Aetna, and August Vlak at Unocal. Important special case work was also provided by Josh Olken, Amy McDonald, Sarah Wigglesworth, Quentin Hope, Paul Bromfield, and Michael Thakr.

I received outstanding support from the visual design professionals at Katzenbach Partners LLC, including Stephanie Buckley, Dewey Moss, and Misty Quinn. The administrative support I received throughout the effort from Jimma Grigsby and Tim Haney and their staffs was outstanding as always. Once again, a special vote of thanks goes to my assistant, Debbie Shortnacy, and my personal quality reader/editor, Linda Katzenbach, who have been an integral part of my writing team for many years. These people took a personal, vested interest in the quality of this book. Last but not least, of course, I appreciate the outstanding editing support from John Mahaney and Shana Wingert of Crown Business. Their ideas and suggestions materially strengthened the book, and their flexibility permitted me to incorporate unique sources and insights.

This book is part of a work in progress. My partner, Niko Canner, and I are leading a major research effort to learn more about how institution-building pride can become an integral part of the leadership and management systems of companies whose front-line workforce performance is critical to their competitive advantage and success in the future. We believe strongly in the motivational value of this effort and are grateful to all those who have taken an interest in this work and continue to support our research.

INDEX

accomplishment, money as scorecard of, 53–54
achievement, 2. *See also* individual achievement (IA)
    material possessions showing, 28
Aetna insurance, 103–121
Alcoa, leadership at, 159
alignment approaches, for workforce behaviors, 140
anticipatory pride, 6, 10, 93–94
Armani, Giorgio, 77
aspirations, 14
Association of Consulting Management Engineers (ACME), 7
Avon, P&M at, 143

Bailey, Rita, 147
Bartholomew, Eddie and Jennifer (pseud.), 61–67
behaviors
    for enterprise performance and employee fulfillment, 140
    reinforcing right behaviors, 115–116
    underlying institution-building pride, 94–96
Blank, Arthur, 91
Boston Consulting Group, 78
Bower, Marvin, 4–13, 51, 124–125, 189
brand value, motivation through, 119–120

Burke, Deb, 37–38
business. *See* enterprise
Buttermore, John, 160–161, 164, 167

Capriati, Jennifer, 31–32
Carney, Art, 76–77
Carter, Debbie, 136–137
Cavanagh, Richard, 15
character, 9–10, 15
closed loop of emotional energy, 17, 23–24
code, professional, 7
Colunga, Daniel, 174
commercialization teams, 86–87
commitment, 42–44, 138
community events, pride and, 191–192
compensation, 51, 60. *See also* money
    programs, 47–48
competitive advantage, motivation through, 119–120
competitive position, motivation through, 125
Conrad, Rich, 170
consistency, of leaders, 195–196
courage, 4
Cowger, Gary, 162–163
coworkers, 85–92, 110–111
craftspeople, 79
creativity, at Microsoft, 75
credit, giving to others, 164–167
Credit Suisse, 61

customer satisfaction, motivation
and, 123

Davis Wire Company (California),
77
decentralization, at GM, 154
De Hoyos Muñoz, Hector, 171–174
dotcom craze, money and, 57
Dunlap, "Chainsaw Al," 93

earnings, pride in, 100
economic gain, motivation through,
117–118
ego, 31–32
Ehrenreich, Barbara, 83
emotion(s). *See also* needs; pride-
builders
frontline motivation and, 121
emotional energy. *See* closed loop of
emotional energy
emotional intelligence, 85
employee fulfillment, enterprise
performance and, 138, 140
employees
at Aetna, 110–116
caliber in work groups, 89–90
at Microsoft, 75
motivation of, 121–126
motivation of senior
management and, 116–121
self-serving, 59
type attracted to enterprise,
87–89
Enders, Thomas, 106–107
energy
closed loop of, 17, 23–24
pride-workforce connection and,
17
Enron, lessons from, 29–30
enterprise
legacy and history of, 91
performance and employee
fulfillment, 138, 140
type of employees attracted to,
87–89
entrepreneurial spirit (ES), 143–145

environment
for peak performance, 133–150
pride-building, 63–64, 65–66
ES. *See* entrepreneurial spirit (ES)
evaluation, rankings through, 50–51
excellence, Peters and Waterman on,
188
executives. *See* senior management
experiences, motivation and, 38–44

family events, pride and, 191–192
Farmer, Amy, 164–167, 191
Fast Company, 148
Faught, Bob, 184
"Feed forward" notion, 93–94
Field, Van, at Unocal, 182
Fifth Dimension, The (Senge), 135
five paths to motivation, 141–149
Flint, Michigan, GM strike in, 155
Fludd, Charlotte, 94–96
Ford, Tom, 77
frontline employees, 121–130
Fry, Art, 145–146

Gardner, Howard, 193–194
Gates, Bill, employees and, 75
General Motors (GM)
aspirations of, 155–156
customer satisfaction at, 123
early influences in, 39–44
giving credit to others at,
164–167
localization at, 190–191
manufacturing scorecard at,
161–164
motivators at, 154–177
pride-builders at, 24–25
process and metrics at, 160–164
respect for what came before,
167–171
simple themes at, 174–177
Toledo Accord and, 43–44
global scaling, at GM, 154
GMI (General Motors Institute), 167
goals, personal and company, 26
Goldsmith, Marshall, 93

Goleman, Daniel, 85
Gordon, Al, 11
GSI (Guest Satisfaction Index), at
    Marriott, 80

health maintenance organizations
    (HMOs), 104, 108–109
heroes, 191
Hewlett-Packard, 124, 196
high performance, managers,
    frontline supervisors, and, 128
Hills Pet Nutrition Company,
    135–137, 138
history, of enterprise, 91
Holt, Tim, 117
Home Depot, 36, 91, 139, 144–145
Hresko, Jamie, 165–166, 167–171,
    192
humor, 15

improvement, continuous, 175–177
incentives. See also specific types
    monetary, 48–53, 55–56,
        196–197
individual achievement (IA),
    145–146. See also achievement
    ego and, 31
    wealth and, 30
individuals, money and ego
    motivation of, 60
individual skill development, 26
indoctrination programs, 84
influence
    on institution-building pride,
        39–44
    as management motivation,
        118–119
innovation, companies exhibiting, 48
institutional values, personal values
    and, 82–84
institution-building (intrinsic) pride,
    16, 18, 26, 32–38, 52. See
    also self-serving pride
    frontline employees and,
        126–130
    fundamentals and, 38–44

instilling, 71–96
vs. money, 139
overlooking, 92–94
sources of, 73–76
integrity, 182
intrinsic pride. See institution-
    building (intrinsic) pride

J. D. Powers Award, to GM, 164
job quality, monetary value of job
    and, 55
Johnson, George, 170
Johnson Space Center (NASA), 122
Jones, Lee, 169
Jordan, Michael, 189

KFC, 140
    pride at, 63–64, 65–66, 80–81,
        147–148, 149
    self-discipline at, 82
"killer apps," 48, 78

labor unions. See also United Auto
        Workers (UAW)
    workforce commitment and,
        42–44
Lansing plant (GM), 164–165
leadership
    enterprise performance,
        employee fulfillment, and,
        138
    in GM system, 156–160,
        177–178
    in Marines, 71–73
    pride and, 2–3, 92–93, 139, 185
    in professional firm, 7
    rotation of, 195–196
leading indicators, for simplifying
    tasks, 194–195
Leading Minds: An Anatomy of
    Leadership (Gardner),
    193–194
lean manufacturing, at GM, 168
legacy of enterprise, 91
lifestyle, money and, 50, 62
localization of pride, 186, 189–193

management. *See* leadership; middle management; senior management; specific enterprises

Manufacturing Managers Council (GM), 24–25, 160–164

Marcus, Bernie, 91, 139

Marine Corps
 discipline, pride, and, 33–35
 localization of pride in, 192–193
 at Parris Island, 35, 198–199
 recruit boot camp of, 84
 role models in, 139
 self-discipline in, 82
 Warrior Stations in, 188

market position, as motivation, 119–120

Marriott, 80, 149

Maslow, Abraham, needs hierarchy of, 27

materialism, 50
 dotcom craze and, 57
 greed, self-serving behaviors, and, 60–61

materialistic pride, 57–58

material possessions, 4, 27–28. *See also* wealth

McKinsey & Company, Inc., 4, 5–13, 50–52, 88–89, 124–125, 189

McQuirter, Paul, 157–158, 159–160, 194, 195

measurement
 at Hills Pet Nutrition Company, 136–137, 138
 at Unocal, 183

mediocre performance, 58

memories, stimulating, 188

metrics of performance. *See* measurement; process and metrics (P&M)

Mexico, GM assembly plant in, 171–174

Microsoft
 employee motivation at, 127–128, 139
 sources of pride at, 73–76

middle management, Williams, Brian, and, 112–116

Minner, Tyree, 175

mission, values, and collective pride (MVP), 141–142

monetary incentives, short-term nature of, 58–59

money, 18, 28. *See also* self-serving pride
 acceptable mediocrity of workforce and, 58
 diversion through, 48–49
 employee motivation and, 128
 as incentive, 48–53
 as indicator of good job, 55
 as initial motivating force, 57–58
 vs. institution-building (intrinsic) pride, 139
 lifestyle and, 50
 motivational limits of, 61–67
 overreliance on, 196–197
 performers and nonperformers separated through, 54–55
 as scorecard of accomplishment, 53–54
 self-serving employees and, 59
 for upper-level vs. lower-level employees, 59–60

Morgan, J. P., Bank, 49

Morton, Dean, 124

motivation. *See also* pride; pride-builders
 at Aetna insurance, 103–121
 through compensation, 47–48
 early experiences and, 38–44
 elements linking pride with, 134–135
 five paths for, 141–149
 at General Motors, 154–177
 at levels within hierarchy, 102
 limits of money for, 61–67
 at Microsoft, 73–76
 performance defined and, 48–53
 pride and, 14–15, 16–19, 23–24
 self-serving materialistic, 51
 of senior management, 117–121

of teams, 90–91
themes of, 186–187
values and, 12–13
wealth as, 30
Murray, Wick, 34
MVP. *See* mission, values, and
    collective pride (MVP)

Nardelle, Robert, 91
needs, 27–29
New United Motor Manufacturing
    Inc., 168
New York City Transit Authority,
    128–129
noble purpose, MVP and, 142
nonmonetary motivation, 62
Novak, David, 149

obstacles, overcoming at GM,
    174–177
O'Neill, Paul, at Alcoa, 159,
    194–195
Owens, John, 86

P&M. *See* process and metrics
    (P&M)
Parker, Gary Lee, 157–158,
    159–160, 195
Parris Island boot camp, 35, 198–199
pay for performance, 47
Payne, Daniel, 183–184
Peak Performance (Katzenbach), 86,
    134
Pearson, Andy, 148
peer approval, 124–125
PepsiCo, 148
performance, 17, 47
    closed loop of emotional energy
        in, 23–24
    employee fulfillment and, 138
    generation through pride, 24–25
    GM tracking of, 160–164
    institution-building pride and,
        198
    mediocre, 58
    money and, 48–53, 54–55

peak environments for, 133–150
personal goals, company goals and,
    26
personal power, wealth and, 30
personal relationships, respect in, 14
personal values, institutional values
    and, 82–84
Peters, Tom, 188, 194
pitfalls
    avoiding, 186–187
    of pride eroders, 195–197
Pontiac, Michigan, GM plant in,
    156–158
position, as management motivation,
    118–119
Post-It notes™, 145–146
power, as management motivation,
    118–119
Powers Award. *See* J. D. Powers
    Award
pride, 32–38. *See also* institution-
    building (intrinsic) pride;
    motivation; self-serving pride
    anticipatory, 6, 10
    in celebrating right things,
        112–116
    employee motivation and, 128
    in how you work, 79–85
    in kind of work, 78–79
    at Microsoft, 73–76
    pitfalls and, 195–197
    respecting what came before
        and, 170–171
    in results of work, 76–79
    sources of, 185
    in *whom* you work with and for,
        85–92
pride-builders
    environment for, 63–64, 65–66
    at GM, 24–25, 153–177
    list for encouraging, 186–197
problem-solving continuous
    improvement, at GM,
    175–177
process, at Hills Pet Nutrition
    Company, 136–137

process and metrics (P&M), 142–143
    at GM, 160–164
"process work," 78
product
    attributes of, 122–123
    pride in, 74–75, 77–78
productive activities, 139–140
professional firm, leadership in, 7
project teams, at Microsoft, 75
purpose, 14

quality performance, at General
        Motors, 44
quantico, Virginia, Marines at,
        34–35, 71–73

Ramos Arizpe, Mexico, GM at,
        171–174
rankings, money and, 50–51
rational compliance, 129–130, 136,
        138
Real Change Leaders (Katzenbach),
        128
recognition and celebration (R&C),
        147–149
recruiting, at Hills Pet Nutrition,
        136–137
reputation, of enterprise, 122
respect
    in personal relationships, 14
    for what came before, 167–171
return on capital, as motivation, 118
role models, 139, 191
Rowe, Jack, 104, 105, 109
Ryan, John, 71–73

safety, at GM, 156–160, 166
salary, role of, 5
Schlichting, Rich, 109–112
scorecard, at GM, 161–164
screening, of employees, 88
self-discipline, 32–33
    work methods and, 81–82
self-serving materialism, 51
self-serving pride, 18, 26, 29–32, 52
    advantages of, 53–56

pitfalls of, 56–61
Senge, Peter, 135
senior management, motivation of,
        116–121
service attributes, motivation and,
        122–123
Shoemaker, Dick, 163
simplicity
    of messages, 186
    of themes, 193–195
Sloan, Alfred, 154
small-team concept, at GM, 168–169
Smith, Douglas K., 49
Snell, Edward, 99–102
software. *See* Microsoft
Sony, Dream Team at, 89–90
Southwest Airlines, 140, 147, 149
    employees of, 87–88
    motivation at, 127–128
    self-discipline at, 82
    training and indoctrination at,
        84
    wealth accumulation and, 36
Spitters, Larry, 4
stock ownership, 127, 196–197
strategic problems, vs. process work,
        78–79
success, 3–4, 17
sustainable competitive advantage,
        119–120
Sutton, Rick, 190

talent, at Microsoft, 75
teams, 26
    caliber of people in, 89–91
    GM small-team concept and,
        168–169
    at KFC, 65–66
    at Microsoft, 75
    motivation of, 60, 90–91
    performance and, 49–50
    at 3M, 86–87
themes
    for overcoming obstacles,
        174–177
    simple, 174–177, 193–195

Thomas, Harvey G., 175, 181
Thompson, David, 181–185, 191
3M, 86, 145–146
titles, for employees, 59–60
Toledo Accord, between GM and
    UAW, 43–44
top-down influence, 10
top-management consulting, 6–7, 8.
    See also Bower, Marvin
tradespeople, 79
training programs, 84
Tricon, 148

UAW-GM Quality Network, 155
union events, pride and, 191–192
United Auto Workers (UAW),
    General Motors and, 43–44,
    157–158, 160–161
United We Stand (Wilber and
    Weekley), 44
Unocal, 181–185, 195
upper management. *See* senior
    management

Vail Ski School, 144
value-driven approach, 141
values
    at Aetna insurance, 103–104
    inculcating, 12–13
    materialism and, 52
    personal and institutional, 82–84
    at Unocal, 183–184
virtue, 2
Vlak, Gus, 156

Wal-Mart, 83
Waterman, Robert, 188
wealth. *See also* material possessions;
    money; self-serving pride
    accumulation opportunity,
        36–37
    needs and, 28–29

pride in, 100
Weekley, Tom, 39–40, 41–44
Wheeler, Richard, 107–108
Wilber, Jay, 39–44
Williams, Brian, 112–116
Williams, Ron, 104–105
Wilmington Car Assembly Plant
    (GM), 174–177
Wisdom of Teams, The (Smith),
    49–50
Woods, Tiger, 189
work
    environment, 153–178
    flows, 136–137
    "how" of, 79–85
    kind of, 78–79
    results of, 76–79
    whom you work with and for,
        85–92
work ethic, 84–85
workforce
    closed loop of emotional energy
        in, 23–24
    commitment of, 42–44
    motivation of, 129–130
    paying more than competition
        and, 58
workforce performance, 17
work group. *See also* teams
    caliber of people in, 89–91
    composition of, 124
workplace
    institution-building pride and,
        38–44
    motivators for, 186–197
    peak performance environment
        in, 133–150
Xavier, Anil (pseud.), 30–31

Zallone, Martin, 100–102
Zubkas, Jim, 170

ABOUT THE AUTHOR

Jon R. Katzenbach is senior partner of Katzenbach Partners LLC, a consulting firm in New York City that specializes in leadership, team, and workforce performance. He is the author of several articles and books, including *Peak Performance, Teams at the Top, Real Change Leaders, The Discipline of Teams* (with Douglas K. Smith), and the bestseller *The Wisdom of Teams* (also with Douglas K. Smith). Before founding Katzenbach Partners LLC, he was a director with McKinsey & Company, Inc. for over thirty years.